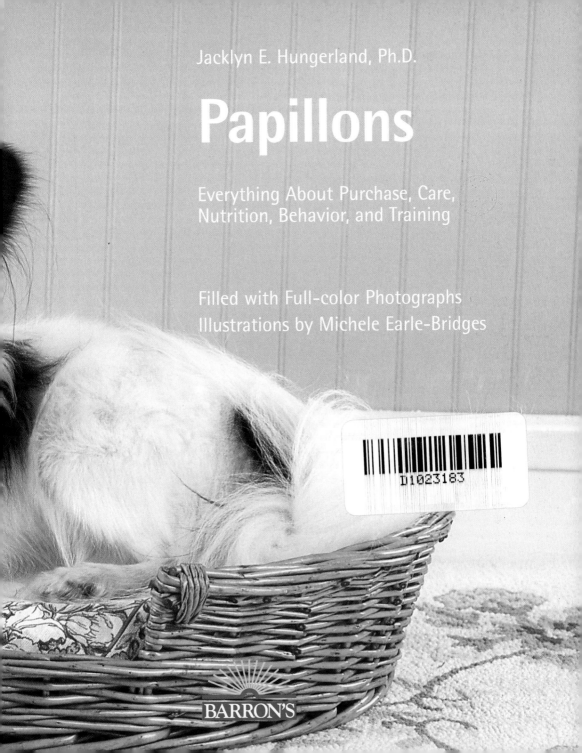

Jacklyn E. Hungerland, Ph.D.

Papillons

Everything About Purchase, Care,
Nutrition, Behavior, and Training

Filled with Full-color Photographs
Illustrations by Michele Earle-Bridges

BARRON'S

2 CONTENTS

PAPILLON HISTORY

A certain bit of romance is attached to the somewhat unclear origins of the Papillon. Papillon owners, including kings and queens, cared less about the details of the Papillon's origins than about their desire for a pretty, dainty lapdog. To this day, the Papillon remains true to that heritage.

Origin of the Breed

When is a dog a butterfly? When it is a Papillon (pronounced pap-ee-yawn), which is the French word for *butterfly*. The name comes from the appearance of the dog's large, obliquely set ears. When fringed with hair, they resemble the waving wings of a butterfly as the dog twitches them back and forth. Not all Papillons have upright ears; some have drooping ears that lie close to the head. This ear type is called Phalene. Pronounced fay-leen by Americans and fah-len by the French, the name was taken from the resemblance of the dog's drop ears to the folded wings of a night moth. Even though the erect-eared Papillon is more commonly seen today, the Phalene was the original type of this elegant toy breed.

The exotic Papillon is both beautiful and fascinating. A loving companion, this pretty lapdog enjoys the admiration of fanciers all over the world.

Throughout this book unless there is a specific reference to a Phalene, the word *Papillon* will cover both forms of the breed.

Where did it come from? There is ongoing debate about where the Papillon first developed because countries often take credit for the origins of popular breeds. Most modern breeds resulted from existing breeds interbred to create the kind of dog people wanted. Some toy dogs were bred down from larger breeds to meet a demand for the qualities of the larger breed in a smaller, more convenient package.

Theories relate the Papillon's development to that of the Maltese, the Japanese Chin, the Chihuahua, and other toys. The common factors linking these breeds with the Papillon are their small size and loving temperament, which won them the favor and demand of sixteenth-century aristocracy and royalty. Some historians believe that if people of privilege had not taken an interest in small dogs, the Papillon might not have survived. Eventually, pretty

The Phalene is the drop-eared variety of the Papillon and takes its name from the folded wings of the night moth.

Papillon of today—a sweet, loving, vivacious, and happy lapdog.

There was such a continued demand in court circles for these spaniels that an enterprising commercial trader from Bologna developed a good business trading the Continental Toy Spaniels back and forth among Italy, Spain, France, and Belgium. Breeders of these spaniels intensified their breeding programs, developing dogs with finer bones, more abundant coats, and profuse feathering. Prices were very high, which is why the Continental Toy Spaniels tended to be the pets of the nobility.

little dogs formed an active type of gift exchange among political and royal figures of the day. That exchange, along with the trading of dogs by sailors, was how various breeds became distributed throughout Europe and the British Isles.

A link in its development: By the sixteenth century, small spaniels existed all over Europe. Those developed from the Dwarf Belgian Spaniels, which were given the more glamorous name of Continental Toy Spaniel, which distinguished them from the English Toy Spaniel-type breeds. The Continental Toy Spaniels depicted in the art of that era closely resemble the Phalene of today, providing a firm link in the Papillon's chain of development.

In sixteenth-century England, Phalene-like dogs were called *Spaniel Gentle* or *Comforter*. Comforter is probably the best single word describing the nature and personality of the

The Papillon in Fine Art

Much of what is known about the history of the Papillon comes from portraits of the nobility. Almost every lady of distinction in the sixteenth century was shown in her portrait with a Phalene-like dog in her lap. Madame Pompadour, a favorite of Louis XV, had two pet Phalenes named Inez and Mimi. At one time there was a painting in the Louvre showing the sister-in-law of Louis XVI holding a perfect Phalene.

The sixteenth-century master, Titian, depicted one version of the Continental Toy Spaniel that showed a clear relationship to the small spaniel breeds with the characteristic high and wide-set, drooping ears, much like those of the Phalene. Many sixteenth- and seventeenth-century paintings showed very similar spaniels. Such evidence suggests the Continental Toy Spaniel was established as a purebred, by the end of the seventeenth century, providing a pretty, smart, and loving pet for the upper classes.

In the late seventeenth century, a Danish Princess (Eleonora) bought a toy spaniel from Bologna, and in 1679, Abraham Wuchters painted her portrait with this dog. The dog was tiny and lightly marked. It had a pretty head with a thin, white blaze. The princess later became the wife of King Charles XI of Sweden, where she continued to favor the tiny spaniels. Two of her spaniels were painted by Ehrensrahl in 1689. This painting, which hangs in the Gripsholm Castle in Sweden, shows the two little dogs with their color, markings, and tail plumes plus their distinctively Phalene heads, leaving no doubt about their heritage.

It is through these paintings of the old masters that we can trace the true foundations of the dog known as the Papillon.

Color and Markings

The Continental Toy Spaniel was usually solid colored with only small touches of white. That fashion lasted for decades. By the sixteenth century, though, some of Titian's paintings showed dogs that were mostly white with red markings. The red-and-white dogs featured in his paintings started a preference for the flashy, evenly marked, spotted dog, and they were referred to as Titian spaniels. Other markings at that time varied from lemon to deep mahogany, and some were black and white or gray and white, depending on the breeder's preference. However, only the red-and-white dog was called a Titian.

TIP

The Current AKC Papillon Standard

"Color—Always parti-color or white with patches of any color(s). On the head, color(s) other than white must cover both ears, back and front, and extend without interruption from the ears over both eyes. A clearly defined white blaze and noseband are preferred to a solidly marked head. Symmetry of facial markings is desirable. The size, shape, placement, and presence or absence of patches of color on the body are without importance. Among the colors there is no preference, provided nose, eye rims and lips are well pigmented black."

Without explanation other than fancy, toward the end of the nineteenth century, the vogue was again for solid colors, with only the feet and chest splashed with white. This style lasted until the late 1920s when a preference for evenly marked, spotted dogs returned. Once the parti-color style was reestablished and set down in the American Kennel Club (AKC) breed standard, it remained for both the Phalene and the Papillon.

The Butterfly Emerges

Even though the Phalene Continental Toy Spaniel had drooping ears, occasionally dogs appeared with ears that stood erect. A few eighteenth-century paintings clearly portray them. This erect ear carriage became fashionable toward the end of the ninteenth century. Breeders turned their efforts to breeding more

Here are good examples of the desirable markings, ear carriage, and expression of a Papillon. As long as color appears where the breed standard specifies, any color is accepted, as can be seen in these examples of a tri-color, a sable, and a black and white.

opposite top: Notice the two disqualifying faults on this red and white Papillon: He is mismarked (color not covering both eyes) and has one ear that failed to become or stay erect. This does not eliminate him from some show activities (see "Showtime! Papillons Do It All"), nor from being loved and loving.

Papillons have always been superlative people dogs.

The Papillon's abundant assets make the breed new friends every day.

Papillon is French for "butterfly," and refers to the similarity of the ears in the erect-eared form of the breed to this most elegant of insects.

by the AKC was a female named Joujou. The year was 1915.

A parent club for the breed, the Papillon Club of America, was founded in 1930 and was recognized by the AKC in 1935. The club held its first national specialty in 1936, after which the club's activities all but discontinued until they were reactivated in 1948. A second specialty was held in 1954 and has continued annually. A parent club is responsible for writing the standard for the breed and caring for the general welfare of the breed.

of these dogs to meet a changing demand. That is when the butterfly wings caused the breed to be called Papillon. From the beginning of the twentieth century in most countries, both ear types have been covered by the Papillon name. An exception is Sweden where Papillon and Phalene are recognized and registered as separate breeds.

The popularity of the Papillon in the United States continues to rise. In 1997, only 2,914 Papillons were registered with the AKC. Since then, registrations have increased steadily but slowly by more than 156 percent to 4,547 registrations in 2002, at which time the Papillon was thirty-eighth in popularity among the 150 breeds recognized by the AKC.

Coming to the United States

In the 1920s, some ladies in England imported Papillons from continental Europe. They formed a breed club and began to breed Papillons quite seriously and quite well. Some of their dogs were exported to the United States. The more frequent appearance of these dogs boosted their appeal to pet owners.

Even though the Phalene was popular for several hundred years in other countries, the Papillon did not become recognized in England or the United States until the beginning of the twentieth century. The first Papillon registered

Some good news: In spite of the Papillon's royal history, a person does not need to be privileged or royal to own and be loved by a member of this delightful breed. Breeders do protect their dogs and puppies, and they are careful about selling Papillons. If you have a good place for the dog to live and a heart that is ready to receive the tireless devotion a Papillon will give, you have a very good chance of finding just the right Papillon for you.

Illustrated Standard

① Round eyes
② Small rounded head with fine muzzle
③ Ears erect or dropped
④ Long tail carried arched over body and covered with a long plume

❑ **Color:** white with patches of any color
❑ **DQ:** over 12" in height, all white dog or dog with no white

Papillon Standard Highlights

The Papillon is small, friendly, and elegant and is distinguished from other breeds by its beautiful butterfly-like ears. It is about 8 to 11 inches (20 to 28 cm) tall at the withers (top of the shoulder blades) and anything over 12 inches (30 cm) is not allowed in conformation shows. The ears, which are so important in defining a Papillon or a Phalene, must either be erect and held at an angle of about 45 degrees or be completely down. The coat is abundant, long, fine, and silky. The coat flows straight and lies flat on the back and sides of the body. However, there is a profuse frill on the chest, and the tail is covered with a long, flowing plume. There is no undercoat.

The Papillon's Place in the Dog World

Papillons are members of the AKC's toy group, which is one of the seven groups of breeds that are categorized according to their size or function. All of the dogs in the toy group are meant to be loving lapdogs, and the Papillon excels in this virtue as it has for centuries.

The Papillon's recent increase in popularity has been helped by the fact that television coverage of dog shows has increased and a Papillon, Champion Loteki Supernatural Being, was seen winning Best In Show at New York's Westminster Kennel Club show in 1999. Kirby, as this dog is known, went on to win the World Dog Show in Helsinki, Finland, and the Royal Invitational Show in Canada, that same year, making him a triple-sweep winner. Kirby, with his special appearance and attitude, enticed the public and has charmed increasing numbers of dog lovers.

A kennel mate of Kirby's, Champion and Obedience Champion Loteki Sudden Impulse, is the most AKC-titled dog of any breed. He holds the top obedience, tracking, and agility titles offered at his time of showing.

The public has discovered, as you will, that the breed is lovable and attractive for city or country dwellers due to its beauty, intelligence, health, and easy care.

CONSIDERATIONS BEFORE YOU BUY

The urge to own a puppy can come over someone without warning. The danger lies in reaching for the want ads to search for a puppy to buy that same day. This is not the best approach, as you will not know much about any puppies you might see. There are never any guarantees. However, finding a responsible breeder can lead you to a better chance of a successful search.

Is the Papillon the Right Dog for You?

Before you consider the Papillon as a companion, you need to decide whether the breed fits into your lifestyle and home. Consider also whether or not you are willing to commit the time and resources necessary to train, groom, and exercise this active breed.

Plan ahead. Finding a Papillon to buy may not be easy. Start contacting breeders because

This child has been taught how and where to interact with her Papillon puppy. She is on the ground and being considerate when holding or playing with a puppy. This is an unusual child, as she has had proper supervision and training on being with her Papillon.

you will likely be put on a waiting list. You will have to be patient if you want to come home with the Papillon of the age and sex you want (see "Selecting Your Papillon").

Papillons' personalities: Papillon owners are dedicated and have a certain passion about the breed. They will tell you that the breed has a beauty and a wonderful temperament, which are absolutely essential qualities. Papillons are happy and friendly and have an outgoing outlook on life. This zest for life tends to rub off on their owners. Papillons are fun and funny and like to be the center of attention. They are very attuned to their owner's feelings and moods and will dream up antics to amuse their owners.

Papillons can be very poised, but they are curious and will explore. They are happy to meet new people, travel on new adventures, and meet new training challenges. They like

The Toy Breeds

Affenpinscher	Manchester Terrier (Toy)
Brussels Griffon	Miniature Pinscher
Cavalier King Charles Spaniel	Papillon
	Pekingese
Chihuahua	Pomeranian
Chinese Crested	Poodle (Toy)
English Toy Spaniel	Pug
Havanese	Shih Tzu
Italian Greyhound	Silky Terrier
Japanese Chin	Toy Fox Terrier
Maltese	Yorkshire Terrier

to snuggle into their owner's lap or bed, but they have to be taught not to jump off of beds or high places because, although they are sturdy, they *can* break.

Papillons are energetic and active, and they live each day to the fullest. They need to have an owner who understands this need for activity. Nothing is halfway with a Papillon. They tend to continue their active lifestyle into their teens. They will chase anything—a ball, a squirrel, a mouse, a butterfly, or even an inviting shadow.

Papillons are very intelligent and can manipulate their owners into letting them do what they want. They can be spoiled easily. Remember that Papillons have a sporting dog heritage and they love to retrieve, so an owner might be seduced into seemingly endless games of fetch.

Many Papillons have catlike behaviors. They like to sit up in high places (but keep an eye on that) or hide under the furniture. They use their paws to wash their faces and lie on their backs to play with toys held in their paws as cats do. Some will catch mice.

Serious Considerations

Even though it is hard to imagine, there might be reasons why the Papillon would not be for you. These things must be considered before you make your decision about getting a Papillon.

Your lifestyle. While they are active and are game for anything you might want to do, Papillons are not great hikers or joggers. You have to remember that you have long legs— they have little legs. That does not match. They are, after all, a toy breed.

Papillons are not wimps, but they are not the kind of dog to ride in the back of a pickup truck. They might even be blown away! They tend to be unaware that they are small, so they will take on anything and anyone. That may lead to problems if large or aggressive animals are in the house or neighborhood. The Papillon might decide to play with or challenge those animals, and the outcome might be disastrous for your dog.

The Papillon is not for you if you expect it to sleep in the garage, the basement, or outdoors. Aside from the fact that they are toy dogs and need to be treated accordingly, the Papillon would be heartbroken to be relegated to any of those conditions. Just do not do it.

Little children: If you have small children in your household, you might reconsider your choice of a Papillon. Papillons are not meant for roughhousing. If there is to be any interaction with small children, it must be monitored until the child is taught how to behave safely with the dog.

Time together: There is one negative thing about Papillons. They are difficult to house-train. Successful house-training depends on the owner, not the dog. It takes time and a lot of patience. The use of a crate as the dog's

If you are considering a Papillon as a companion, do the required research to be sure this is the right breed for you. There is considerable reading material available to help you as well as many Internet web sites devoted to the breed.

personal space will be a help in house training if you commit to using it. (See "At Home with Your Papillon.")

Training time should not be the only together time for you and your dog. Papillons need, adore, and want to please you, and they need and want you to adore them. They need *time* with you. They need to play games with you such as retrieving and doing tricks. They are happy going to training or socialization classes or just going for a little walk, as long as it is time spent with you. They want to be tucked up next to you when you read the paper or have your evening relaxation time. Actually, they want to be attached to you as if with Velcro. If this does not appeal to you, you may not be right for a Papillon.

The Commitment

You may have decided that you want a Papillon, but you must want to give the dog the care, attention, training, and love she deserves. Having a dog is a serious responsibility. Over the years of her life, your companion will rely on you for attention, proper nutrition, training, good health care, proper living conditions, and lots of love. There are also financial responsibilities if you are to provide these things with quality.

Timing is important: Papillon breeders are very conservative about the number of puppies

they produce. They are selective about selling their Papillons, too. Responsible breeders want to be sure that their puppies or adults will be going to a home that is appropriate for them. A stable environment is very important for a newcomer. Stability includes being sure who will be the dog's primary caretaker. Papillons need to know who their people are. They need to know who is the one they can turn to and from whom they can expect the love they need.

If you plan to go off to work and leave your new Papillon alone, the chance is that the dog will become bored. Boredom leads to bad habits, such as chewing, barking, and failure to mind the house-training rules. Try to adjust household schedules so that someone will be with the dog for most of the day.

The wrong times: Anytime there is stress in the household is not the time to bring a Papillon home. If you are moving, going on vacation, changing jobs, having a new baby, divorcing, or facing any other event that will upset the balance of the household, this is not

above: Patience is essential in finding a Papillon puppy. Litters are usually small and breeders are normally very careful about where their puppies are placed.

left: Taking a nap on his favorite chair, this puppy seems to say: "Please leave me alone. I'm new here and I'm exhausted from exploring this new territory. Call me at dinnertime."

above: If your sole purpose in owning a Papillon is to enjoy a delightful pet, plan to have it neutered. Breeding dogs, especially toy breeds, is fraught with problems. Additionally, pet overpopulation is a serious problem and no real dog lover should want to swell the numbers.

right: A good example of the breed standard is presented in this picture of a young dog. His markings are quite nice, he has good proportion between height and length of body, and his coat appears to be single and silky. Note his nice feet and his moderate ear fringes.

the time for more stress. The addition of a new puppy or dog can be stressful for you and for the animal. Newcomers require more time and attention.

One of the worst times to bring home a new pet is on a holiday. Holidays are times of excitement, and that usually leads to a lot of activity and disruption in the household. Too often people want to buy a dog as a surprise gift. This would be a huge mistake. One of the most important things in acquiring a Papillon is whether or not the person and the dog connect. You cannot make that decision for another person or for a Papillon.

The best thing to do if you are absolutely sure a Papillon would be an appropriate and welcome gift is to get a photograph of a litter of Papillon puppies and include the picture in a greeting card. That way the recipient can be excited and the Papillon will not get lost in the shuffle of holiday activities. After the holiday, the recipient can go to the breeder's location

---

TIP

Benefits of Neutering
- ✔ Prevents pet overpopulation
- ✔ Prevents estrus and its inconveniences
- ✔ Prevents unwanted pregnancies
- ✔ Prevents reproductive tissue diseases
- ✔ Prevents testicular cancer
- ✔ Reduces the chance of developing mammary cancer
- ✔ Requires less surgical procedure time
- ✔ Allows quicker healing

---

and make that special connection with a Papillon.

Should Your Papillon Be Neutered?

An important decision you will have to make about your Papillon is whether or not to have it neutered and when. Spaying (of females) and castrating (of males) are called neutering. They are surgical procedures that remove some or all of the reproductive tissues in the dog's body. In the male, the testicles are removed. In the female, the ovaries and uterus are removed.

The age at which neutering should occur has been the source of controversy among veterinarians and dog breeders and fanciers. Breeders of Papillons are reluctant to have their dogs anesthetized unless it is absolutely necessary, due to the breed's sensitive reactions to the type and amount of anesthetics. If surgery is a necessity, breeders are willing to invest in a costly anesthetic called isoflurane rather than risk allergic reactions their Papillons have experienced with the more commonly used anesthetics.

To avoid surgery, breeders prefer to tolerate the inconvenience of a female's estrus (called a *season* or *heat*). During this time, vaginal bleeding occurs that can stain furniture and carpets and that attracts males to the female. Responsible breeders take precautions to prevent unplanned breedings in their own females and in the females they sell for breeding or show.

When females or males are not to be used for breeding, responsible breeders require completion of a spay/neuter contract from purchasers. Papillon breeders will recommend neutering after the female's first (carefully supervised) estrus or at about the age of six months for males and females. A spay/neuter contract is a written agreement between buyer and seller to the effect that registration papers will not be furnished to the buyer until the seller has evidence that the dog has been neutered or spayed. Often the contract specifies a date or age by which neutering must take place. It is important that the agreement be signed by the buyer before leaving the seller's premises.

Some sellers like to have buyers enter into a co-ownership contract with buyer and seller having equal control over the life of and decisions regarding the dog. No matter how appealing the offer may seem, co-ownerships too often lead to problems and legal disputes, and these contracts are not recommended.

Veterinarians have a different point of view about neutering. Initially, neutering was an approach to control animal overpopulation, an approach that has had positive effects with fewer unwanted dogs and, especially, cats. Research has been able to connect a reduction in the incidence of mammary cancer and a prevention of reproductive tissue diseases to early spaying and neutering. Veterinarians encourage and endorse spaying prior to a female's first estrus (and definitely prior to a second estrus) and neutering of males as early as six weeks of age.

Discuss neutering with your veterinarian and the breeder from whom you bought your Papillon. Their input will help you decide the best course of action for your Papillon's health and your lifestyle.

SELECTING YOUR PAPILLON

*Once you have decided you want to
own a Papillon, questions will
race through your mind. Will I be
a good owner? Will I have enough
time to give to the puppy? The
way you select your Papillon
must be a careful process. A good
start promises a good relationship.*

Where to Find a Papillon

Check out the Papillon Club of America's
(PCA) and the American Kennel Club's (AKC)
web pages (see "Information") for information,
breeder referrals, and locations of dog clubs in
your area. If you attend some club meetings,
you are likely to meet breeders, trainers, and
dog fanciers who can give you information
about local Papillon breeders. Dog publications,
usually available at a bookstore or pet shop,
have advertisements placed by breeders with
puppies available or expected. When you have

*This little guy is adorable, isn't he? He
deserves to have your full attention, without
distractions, when you bring him home.
His homecoming should be the "holiday,"
not a day of disruption, noise, and crowds
that are common on human holidays.*

collected sufficient information, it is up to you
to make a judgment about the responsibility of
the breeder you select. Contact the breeder
and set up an appointment to meet and to see
his or her Papillons in their home setting.

A responsible Papillon breeder can tell you
all about the history, health, temperament, and
personalities of the puppies. In most cases, you
will be able to meet the sire and dam of the
litter and the littermates. Responsible breeders
usually follow up after they sell a puppy. You
will also have a built-in mentor—someone who
can answer all your questions and support your
activities with your Papillon.

More Highlights from the Breed Standard

The breed standard describes some details
you will want to look for when searching for

Genetic Anomalies of the Papillon*

Disorder	Test Availability	Type of Treatment
Progressive retinal atrophy	Annual ophthalmic examination	None
Patellar luxation	Manual manipulation	Surgery
Heart anomalies	Veterinary and blood tests	Medication
Hypoglycemia	Blood glucose monitoring; family history	Quick action
Cataracts	Observation; veterinarian exam	Surgery possible
Epilepsy	Incidence; family history	Medication
Retained testicles	Veterinarian examination	None; neutering

*Where any hereditary factors exist, the affected animals should be removed from the breeding pool to prevent perpetuating the disorder(s).

your Papillon. The body should be slightly longer than the height at the shoulder. When you look at the head, you should see dark, round, medium-sized eyes with an alert expression. The head is small with a well-defined stop (like the bridge of your nose) where the muzzle joins the skull. The muzzle is fine, tapering to the nose, which is black, small, rounded, and slightly flat on top. The lips should be tight, thin, and black, and the tongue must not show when the mouth is closed. Teeth must be in a scissors bite.

The neck is of medium length and flows into a straight and level back line. The chest is of medium depth with the ribs well sprung. The shoulders are well developed and are laid back to allow freedom of movement. The hindquarters are also well developed and well angulated. Front and rear feet are thin and elongated (harelike), pointing neither in nor out.

When the Papillon moves, his gait should be free, quick, easy, and graceful. He should not be paddle footed or stiff in his hip movements.

Above all, the Papillon must be happy, alert, and friendly. He should never be shy or aggressive. Disqualifications from conformation competition are a dog standing over 12 inches (30 cm), an all-white dog, or a dog with no white.

Faults that should be noted include small or pointed ears, ears that are set too high, one ear up or ears partly down; a nose that is not black; a bite that is overshot or undershot; a low-set or short tail or a tail that is not arched over the back. It is a serious fault if color other than white does not cover both ears, back and front, or does not extend from the ears over both eyes.

Inherited Health Factors

Looking for a Papillon that conforms to the breed standard is one thing. Finding a Papillon that is beautiful and also has a family that has been monitored for genetic faults may be quite another. Some disorders can be diagnosed and treated. Others may be diagnosable but not treatable. When you search for your Papillon companion, be sure to discuss genetic anomalies (inherited disorders) of the Papillon with the breeder.

The concerned Papillon breeder will have evidence of the appropriate examinations and certifications, if any, of these disorders in the family history. That is the best the breeder can do. You should be aware that genetics is like a game of chance; there are no absolutes. Even if several generations have been free of a disorder, that does not guarantee that the disorder will never occur in your Papillon.

Do not expect to come away with a puppy on the day of your first visit. Use this initial visit to establish a relationship with the breeder and get to know the relatives of your puppy. You might have to go on a waiting list for your Papillon, as demand is high and supply is low. The wait may seem endless but the knowledge that you will be getting a happy, healthy Papillon will make it worthwhile. You are entitled to start out with an outgoing, self-assured, happy, and healthy puppy that meets your expectations and makes you feel satisfied that you selected the Papillon.

Puppy, Adult, or Rescue?

When thinking about getting a dog, most people envision a fuzzy little bundle of cuteness. Papillons stay that way throughout their lives. Papillon puppies have slowly developing and fragile immune systems. They are not weaned until they are eight to ten weeks old. They are not allowed to go to their new homes until they are about 12 weeks of age, a time that is excellent for the puppy's adjustment to his new environment.

If you have little inclination toward raising a Papillon puppy, you might consider looking for a grown dog. Breeders sometimes have older puppies or adult Papillons that need a good

---

TIP

Questions You Should Ask the Breeder

✔ Are the puppies purebred and registered? With which registry?
✔ How long has the breeder been involved with the breed?
✔ Does the breeder belong to a local or the national Papillon club?
✔ How many puppies are available to see?
✔ How old are the available puppies?
✔ Are both parents available to meet? If not, why?
✔ Have the parents been tested for genetic problems? What were the results?
✔ What are the prices of the puppies? If they vary, why?
✔ How many puppies were in your Papillon's litter?
✔ At what age were the puppies weaned?
✔ Have the puppies had a veterinary exam? Worm check?
✔ Have the puppies received inoculations? If so, which ones and at what dosage?
✔ Have the puppies been socialized?
✔ Have the puppies had basic training?
✔ Will you be allowed a 24-hour return option until you can have your puppy examined by your own veterinarian?
✔ What type of documentation will you receive with your puppy?

---

and loving home. The breeder might insist on you signing a contract to neuter the dog if that has not already been done. The reputable

When you visit a breeder, you can expect to meet the puppies' mother. However, if the breeder used an "outside stud," you are unlikely to meet the puppies' father. In that event, ask to see his photo; most breeders will be happy to show you one.

breeder will let you know if there are any problems in the dog's behavior or health as well as any idiosyncracies in his personality.

Most purebred dog organizations have what is called a rescue program for dogs of their breed that have been abandoned, mistreated, or left behind by a passing owner. The PCA has a nationwide rescue program. Rescue dogs come in all ages and sometimes need special care and attention. A rescue Papillon always appreciates a good place to live out his life.

Selecting a Puppy

All puppies are appealing. Your task is to select a puppy using facts, not emotions. You will be seeing the puppies in their home environment, where you can observe their natural behavior. Being able to observe the parents of the puppies is best since most puppies will reflect the temperaments of their parents. The way you raise your Papillon will also affect his personality.

Pretend you are a veterinarian and do your best to evaluate the general health of the puppies. Are they outgoing and running around with no evidence of lameness? Are their eyes

Papillons are good mothers. This female is happy to present her babies to you. Note how healthy Mom is, which is a positive indicator of her family's health and longevity.

With so many ages and personalities to see, which one will you choose? If you don't want the work involved in raising a puppy, there are other options available in adult or rescue dogs, any one of which will be a loving Papillon.

clear and without discharge? Are their ears clean? They should not be shaking their heads or scratching at their ears. Are their gums bright pink? Are their teeth clean and firmly set? Does their skin seem pliable and without rashes? Are their coats shiny? Are the puppies in good weight but without pot bellies? Are there any signs of parasites? Are the puppies warm and happy?

Put yourself on the puppy's level: Sit on the floor. How you react to the puppies' playfulness will influence how the puppies will

This little girl shows us a good example of how to get down to the Papillon puppy's level. It's the best way to get to know the prospective companion that will go home with you.

TIP

Questions the Breeder Will Ask You
✔ Why do you want a Papillon?
✔ What do you know about Papillons and their needs?
✔ How many other dogs do you have at home? What kinds and what ages?
✔ How many children are at home? If so, what ages?
✔ What is your yard like?
✔ Where will the puppy sleep?
✔ When you are away from home, what will happen to the puppy?
✔ Do you want a show dog or a pet? Why?
✔ Do you want a male or a female? Why?

react to you. If you react with a loud voice or a sudden move, the puppies that did not become startled or run away will match your personality most closely.

Sizes: Different Papillon families grow at different rates, so you will have to rely on the breeder's estimate of what sizes the puppies will be when they are adults. If you are buying a Papillon as a show prospect, remember that any dog over 12 inches (30 cm) at the shoulder cannot be shown in AKC conformation events. He may compete in companion events and can be a wonderful service dog or therapy dog. No matter what size, though, your Papillon will be your special companion.

If you are determined to have the erect-eared Papillon, get an older puppy. Some dogs that start out as puppies with erect ears can develop drop ears when they are about one year old and they become Phalenes. Both ear types may occur in the same litter, and the breeder should be able to tell you if this has happened in the family of your prospective puppy. If you take a young puppy, be sure you will love the puppy whether or not he becomes a Phalene.

Male or Female?

Deciding on a male or a female Papillon is a personal preference that might be based on experience with other dogs you have owned. There are personality differences in Papillons, the primary one being that the males tend to be more dependent than the females. If you have some definite preference, be sure to let the breeder know as soon as you can, as it might affect your standing on a waiting list. When you see the Papillons that are available to you, it will not matter to you what sex is available. You will go with the one that steals your heart.

Age and Longevity

Papillons are prone to long life. With proper care and attention to the basics of dental and physical health, they are known to live to 15 years and beyond. Very often longevity is a family characteristic. Check with the person from whom you buy your Papillon to get an idea of how long relatives lived and how their health was in their later years. Select your Papillon with care since you will likely be responsible for that dog for a long time.

Registering Your Papillon

Registration will complete your pride and satisfaction in owning your special Papillon. It will also allow you and your dog to take part in many activities, including conformation, obedience, and agility.

Do not be confused about the differences between a registration certificate and a pedigree. A pedigree should be given to you by the breeder. It is a history of your Papillon's relatives (parents, grandparents, and beyond). A registration certificate is issued by the kennel club and is proof of parentage and proof that your Papillon is a registered purebred. Along with a pedigree, your Papillon's breeder should supply you with a registration certificate.

A pedigree should give you information about your dog and his ancestors. The top half of the page will tell you all the names of your Papillon's sire's family. The bottom half of the page will tell you the same type of information for your dog's dam's family. The names on the pedigree might be preceded by letters denoting championships or followed by letters denoting obedience or agility accomplishments.

Registration: When a breeder sends a litter registration form to the AKC, the AKC will send a kit containing individual intermediate registration forms for each puppy in the litter. This individual form will be what the breeder will use to transfer ownership to you. Your form must be completed within six months and sent to the AKC with the proper fee. You will receive a permanent registration certificate showing you as the owner of your Papillon.

Caution: Do not enter into a purchase in which you can receive registration papers for an additional amount of money. Your purchase should be a straightforward transaction with your Papillon and his documentation forming an inseparable package.

There are established registries other than the AKC (see "Information"). If you are buying your Papillon from a breeder who uses one of those, you should contact that registry for guidance on their registration procedures.

Papillon or Phalene, a healthy, well-bred, properly socialized puppy will be a joy to your life for many years. Starting off right will assure that you get the most out of the experience.

AT HOME WITH YOUR PAPILLON

The big day has arrived. You have done all your homework, and you have found your ideal Papillon. The time has come to bring her home for a happy lifetime. You will want her to feel safe and secure, and you will want to be well-prepared for her arrival.

Your Papillon Comes Home

With any luck, your Papillon will have been introduced to a travel crate before you come to pick her up. There are going to be many times and circumstances when you will want to have her in her crate at home or when traveling. Bring a travel crate with you for her trip home. Ask the breeder for a familiar toy or snuggle pad to put into the crate with the soft blankets and small treat you have provided. This will be comfortable and reassuring for her.

You will be tempted to have this furry bundle sit in your lap for the journey home. One of the problems with that is that she will think like a Papillon and will always expect to sit in your lap after that. It is also unsafe. So put your precious Papillon into her crate.

There is also the risk of her being carsick, especially if this is her first car trip. She might vomit or drool. It is helpful if she has not eaten for at least two hours before you pick her up. Before you put her into the crate, let her relieve herself. Riding in the crate is the safest place for her.

If she cries and fusses in the crate soothe her with a calm voice. You must steel yourself for her complaining, and do not give in to her pleas. She might even be lulled to sleep by the movement of the car.

As they have for centuries, Papillons bring abundant joy to those whose lives they share. Active, intelligent, and with a great desire to please and learn, these dogs give their owners all that could be asked for in an ideal companion dog.

The Arrival

Take the first few days very easy. Give her a chance to check out her new surroundings. Show her where her water bowl is, where you have put her bed or crate, and where she is expected to relieve herself. Do not press her to eat or drink anything. She might be tired from the excitement of the trip and her explorations. Put her into the safe area you have prepared for her (see "Housing Considerations") and leave her alone. If you want to put her into her crate, put some small treats and her familiar toy in the back of the crate to make it worth exploring. Praise her and give her another treat as you close the door of the crate. Be sure she has completely pottied before you put her into her crate. If she tests you with her cries, go into another room or outside until she settles down.

Children: Papillons do not do well with children under the age of eight or ten. Children should not be allowed to tease or be rough with the dog, and they should not be allowed to pick her up. Papillon puppies are wiggly and can fall or leap out of a child's arms easily. If a child wants to play with the dog, let the child sit on the floor. If the puppy is licking the child's face and jumping into the child's lap, the child may be frightened by the dog's behavior and might let out loud shrieks, scaring the puppy. An adult should supervise to prevent injury to the dog or an unfortunate experience for the child.

Other pets: Papillons can be very possessive, and some of them need to be only children. If you have more than one pet, introducing your new puppy has to be handled carefully so that resident dogs or pets do not get jealous. Resident dogs will be curious about the newcomer. There will be nose-to-nose greetings through the openings in the exercise pen around the puppy's safe area. Do a favorite activity with the resident dogs. Pay a lot of attention to them. Give them new toys and special treats. Go for a walk or a ride in the car. Do whatever is necessary to reassure them that they are not being forgotten.

Naming Your Papillon

Naming a dog is like naming a child. It gives her a sense of identity and makes her realize that she is special. Be sure your puppy's name does not sound like any other names in the household, human or pet. This will avoid confusion, especially when your new puppy is trying to learn who she is. Try to choose a name for your puppy that is two syllables and ends with a vowel, as these seem to be easiest for dogs to recognize (for example, Buddy or Poppy). A dog should never be named with anything that rhymes with a training word, most of which are single syllable (*"Sit," "Come," "Down," "Stay"*). Using a two-syllable name will keep you from naming your puppy anything that sounds like one of the training words.

Under proper circumstances, a Papillon can be a good choice as a pet for an older, considerate child. Children in the family must be taught how to respond to a Papillon puppy, and adult supervision should always be a part of any child/puppy interaction.

Start using your Papillon's name as soon as you bring her home and she will soon realize that you are talking to her. Once she learns her name, it will be easy for you to get her attention, which is the first step in training and communicating with her.

Housing Considerations

Papillon puppies are bundles of energy. You might be tempted to let her have free run of the house. However, that would be a mistake that you would regret as soon as there were messes on the carpet and teeth marks on your antique chair leg. She must have a definite area set aside for her safe space that will always feel to her like her personal refuge. This might be an exercise pen, a laundry room, or an area off the kitchen or in the family room. The crate in which she came home should be put into this area so that her level of comfort when in her crate will continue or increase. This should be her permanent housing and sleeping area. Be sure her space allows her to see household activities and people. Isolation and boredom will lead to barking and anxiety and is not good for her. Exposure to the sights, sounds, and smells of the household will be a major part of her socialization.

You have several different housing options. Remember to have all the necessary items in your home before your Papillon arrives.

Crates and kennels: Travel kennels and lightweight, easy-to-clean, well-ventilated solid crates made of plastic, fiberglass, or wire

Most toy dogs have no concept of their own size, so when introducing a Papillon to any larger dog, it is best to closely monitor the dogs.

should be open on all sides. These provide a sense of freedom to your dog.

Exercise pens: Portable, folding wire, or plastic pens are a must. Some even have covers.

Safety gates: Folding or rigid barriers made of plastic or wood must be used to close off areas, stairways, or doorways to control the dog's access or escape and to prevent accidents.

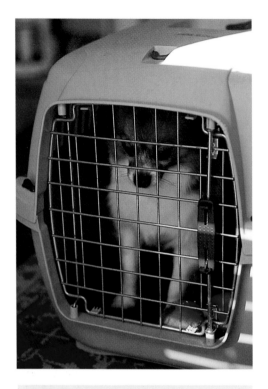

This puppy has crate and will travel. Notice that the crate is just the right size for the puppy. Also notice that the puppy is quite happy to be in the crate, which means that she has become familiar with it. That is a great benefit for you.

Bedding: Sheepskin or sheepskin-like pads, blankets, and snuggle sacks or beds that are machine washable and dryer safe should be within the kennel or crate. This furniture will be rearranged by the Papillon to suit her idea of comfort.

Safety First

Preparing your home before your Papillon's arrival is much like having a human toddler come to visit. You will have to do a thorough check for hazards, including getting down on your knees to check out life from her point of view.

Household cleaning products and chemicals: Check cupboards for open or spilled household cleaners or chemicals. Many of these are potentially deadly for your curious Papillon. Any objects that might have lead-based paint on them can be toxic if she chews on them.

Antifreeze is a major cause of animal poisoning. It is sweet and dogs are attracted to it. However, it is deadly. Your dog needs to ingest only a small amount to cause severe kidney damage. Check your garage floor and your car for traces of antifreeze. If you suspect there is some, do not allow any animals in the garage until it has been cleaned.

Rodent bait and snap traps: Throw away any rodent bait that has been put out for rats or mice. The poison is just as deadly for a Papillon as it is for a small rat. Remember that

---

TIP

The Crate and Safe Area

✔ Never use the crate or the safe area for punishment.

✔ Do not leave your Papillon closed in a crate for any extended time.

✔ Do not buy a crate that is too large.

✔ Put the safe area close to or in a corner of an area with lots of people activity.

✔ Always provide a treat and lots of praise when putting your Papillon into her crate or the safe area.

The new arrival should have plenty of toys and should be left alone to relax and get used to his new surroundings. Be sure he is in his safe place.

Papillons will catch mice. If your puppy should eat a mouse that has died from rodent poison, there is the danger that she will be poisoned, too. Snap traps are almost as bad. Imagine such a trap snapping onto your finger. That is the equivalent of it snapping onto your Papillon's foot or leg (or tail!). Along with pain, there might be a broken bone.

Electrical dangers: When your Papillon is loose in the house, keep an eye on any electrical cords. Puppies love to chew on them. If she chews through the insulation, your Papillon could be electrocuted. It is also possible that sparking wires within the cord might cause a fire.

Kitchen and appliances: Do not have your Papillon loose in the kitchen with you while you are cooking or near you when ironing clothes. This will prevent begging and accidents from spilled hot liquids. There is the remote but possible chance that you might drop a food can or the iron. If one of these should hit your puppy on the head, it could be fatal. Put her in her safe place where she can watch your activity with her natural interest, but in safety.

Doors: When your puppy is loose in the house, make certain that all doors to the out-side or to the garage are guarded with safety

Look beyond this nice Papillon and notice that the fence is in good repair and the spaces between the boards are not large enough for the dog to go through. This looks like a safe place to play ball.

Electrical wires are very attractive— and very dangerous—to young puppies. Be especially vigilant and diligent in teaching your Papillon puppy to stay away from anything electrical.

gates, even if the doors are closed. If someone should open a door from the other side, there is no danger of your puppy escaping into the street where she might be hit by a car or where she might become lost when a gate is in place. Papillons are quick, and she might dash out an open, ungated door faster than you realize.

Injuries: When you walk around with your Papillon loose in the room, you have to learn to do the puppy shuffle, not picking your feet up for fear of stepping on that vulnerable being. This shuffle will also save you from being tripped and thrown off balance by the puppy darting out from nowhere to play a game of chase with you. The shuffle will save you both from painful injuries.

Poisonous plants: Certain indoor and garden ornamental plants are toxic to animals (e.g., ivy and oleander). Keep the indoor plants out of the puppy's reach, and watch her carefully in the garden. Better yet, buy only non-toxic varieties. If you are uncertain about your garden, contact the National Animal Poison Control Center (see "Information").

Foreign objects: Pins, needles, rubber bands, paper clips, parts of childrens' toys, and any small objects on the floor are potential choking

hazards for your Papillon. If she should swallow even a stray penny, there is danger of poisoning from the high zinc content.

Garbage holds some allure for dogs but can be toxic. Be sure your Papillon does not have access to spoiled or decaying food, which contains toxins.

Candies and medicines: Chocolate may be a favorite in the household, but it must be kept securely away from your Papillon. It contains a substance that is similar to caffeine and is toxic to dogs. Other kinds of candies can become stuck in her teeth or throat, causing choking.

You should never leave any kind of medicine where your Papillon can reach it. Common, over-the-counter remedies that you think are harmless can be fatal for your puppy, even in small amounts.

The yard: Your Papillon should never be out in the yard without supervision. An open gate or a hole in the fence is inviting and could lead to her getting out into a dangerous world. Check your fence and gates. Replace loose boards or wires, and make sure gate locks work. Any space that is big enough for your fist to go through is big enough for a Papillon to go through. Fix all gaps. A secure yard will also prevent unwanted animals from coming in.

Identification

The first thing you should do for your Papillon is provide her with some form of permanent identification. If she should get lost, it would be unlikely that you could get her back unless she has proper identification. There is no reason to take such a chance.

A microchip is about the size of a grain of rice. It is easily implanted under the skin by injection. Each chip has a unique number that can be read by a handheld scanner. Microchips are safe, permanent, and cannot be altered. If your Papillon is microchipped, the following information will be entered into a central computer registry:

The chip identification number

Your dog's description

Your name, address, and telephone number

An alternate contact in case you cannot be reached.

In addition, an identification tag for the dog's collar is provided. This indicates her identification number and the registry's telephone number.

The American Kennel Club has the Companion Animal Recovery program that has returned more than 110,000 tattooed or microchipped pets to their owners. A similar program, the National Recovery Service, is sponsored by the Canadian Kennel Club.

Collars and name tags: If you think there is any chance that your Papillon might get out or be lost while you are traveling, you might consider getting her a tag and a collar. Collars and

tags are easily seen and indicate that the dog has a family. Collars and tags are, of course, detachable (in fact, the collar should be a quick-release collar like a cat collar) and can get lost. A more permanent form of identification is better.

A tattoo is a form of permanent identification, as is the microchip. Tattoos can be registered with the AKC or United Kennel Club (UKC) animal recovery programs. Most veterinarians tattoo dogs with a light sedative. On small dogs like the Papillon, a tattoo is usually done on the inner thigh or on the belly. If you plan to have your Papillon tattooed, you might want to have it done at the same time you have her spayed.

Setting up a folding exercise pen for your Papillon puppy in a corner of the kitchen or family room assures that the puppy is both safe and in the midst of family activity. Be sure to include her crate, a bowl of water, and some toys to enhance her "space."

It's best to collect the supplies for your new pet in advance of the homecoming. Notice the toothbrush, paste, and honey (it is necessary to have this on hand at all times), along with bowls, towels, a lead, and some toys.

House-Training Your Papillon

Forget all about *housebreaking,* which is done with a punishment approach. *House-training* methods that provide encouragement and reward are more appropriate. Like young children, dogs cannot remember their lessons until they reach an age when they can understand what you want. For dogs, this is at about 12 weeks of age. You will be getting your Papillon at about that age, so you might think that house-training her will go quickly. Papillons are not easy to house-train because they are so close to the ground and so quick and their coat masks their behavior. They can piddle almost in midstride before you know anything is happening. Success will depend on your alertness, your consistency, and lots of patience.

Two goals of house-training are to teach the dog bladder and bowel muscle control and to get the message across about acceptable places to go potty. This has to be done in very small increments. Until your Papillon is trained, you will have to spend most of your time keep-ing her on schedule and monitoring her behaviors. Carry rewarding treats with you at all times. For a Papillon, very small pieces of treats that can be swallowed quickly work best so that time is not wasted in chewing, which would interrupt the training sequence of behavior/reward.

Your responsibilities: You must be sure she is taken to her relief area after she wakes up, after having been in her crate, after meals, after playing, and before going to bed for the night. Puppies under six months need to go out about every two hours.

The nuts and bolts: Dogs do not like to soil their sleeping quarters, and Papillons are no different. From the very beginning, put your puppy into her crate with the door closed for close to two hours. When you let her out, take her immediately to her potty area, which might be a far corner of her safe area or it might be outside, where she will be on leash. Stay there with her until she does something, and immediately give excited praise and a treat. After that, every time you take her to her potty area, use a command that she will learn means to go potty. In fact, *"Go potty"* is a good command, as is *"Hurry up."* Once you have taken her to her potty area, do not give up on the task until she has gone potty. If you give up, she will still need to potty and will end up making a mistake in the house. If this happens, do not ever scold her. Next time, wait until she is successful in the approved area. As the puppy matures and shows that she is getting some muscle control, gradually increase her crate time, but that should never be all day. If you have to be away for several hours, leave her loose in her safe area, or in her crate if you arrange for a midday dog walker to exercise her.

If you have to go to work, you might decide to train her to use a litter pan. The pan can be in a corner of her safe area as far from her sleeping crate as possible. Another option is commercial pads that are available at your pet store. Some of these pads have odor control and something that attracts the dog to use the pad. Do not use newspapers on the floor because the ink comes off on the pads of the feet and might cause an allergic reaction.

Your Papillon should show signs of getting the message after 10 to 14 days, which all depends on how regular you have been in her training. This may be the time to start having her loose in the house with you. Be sure she is exercised, and supervise her at all times. You may want to have her on a lightweight leash to keep track of her because she will want to explore every inch of the house. Pay close attention to her moves. If she increases her activity, starts sniffing the floor, goes toward her safe area or the door, or shows other signs of an impending accident, take her to her potty area right away and wait for her to potty. Do not forget the praise and the treat after she performs.

CHECKLIST

Grooming Supplies
✔ Grooming table
✔ A good-quality, stainless-steel, snag-free dog comb with medium-spaced teeth
✔ Toenail clippers
✔ Styptic powder
✔ A spray bottle that will give a very fine mist
✔ A soft-bristle toothbrush and toothpaste made especially for dogs
✔ A good tearless shampoo and conditioner
✔ Blunt-nosed scissors

With time and care, your Papillon will begin to relax on the table. This will give you the cue that it is all right to begin grooming, including dental and nail care.

Grooming Your Papillon

The several requirements of grooming are minimal in the Papillon. In spite of their coat being abundant, Papillons are known as a wash-and-wear breed.

Glamour without trouble: A frequent question is "Do they shed?" Papillons tend to shed a little all along with a big shed in the springtime. When this happens, all you have to do is bathe the coat and boost the shed along to its finish. Females, whether they are bred or not, will often shed when puppies they might have had would be about six weeks old.

Equipment and supplies: All grooming is supported by the right kinds of equipment and supplies. Very little grooming equipment is needed for the Papillon. With very little trouble you will have the joy of a well-groomed, glamorous Papillon to amuse and adore you.

Grooming Fundamentals

Using a grooming table will help your dog become accustomed to being examined there and it will make life easier for you and for your veterinarian. Many different types of grooming tables are available through catalogs or at your local pet supply store. Any table or bench will do as long as it has a nonslip surface such as rubber matting. Carpeting is too slippery to stand on.

Caution! Never ever leave your Papillon alone on the table—not even for a second. If you turn away there is always the danger that your dog will jump or fall from the table. That could spell a quick trip to the veterinarian for broken legs or worse. The best policy is to keep one hand on the dog at all times. If you have to leave the table, take her with you or put her into her crate until you can return.

Grooming brush: Your most important grooming tool will be your grooming brush. You will need a very good bristle brush for the red-marked Papillon. The Mason Pearson brush is used by aficionados. This brush is also used on the ears. It is a costly brush but worth the investment. Since the tricolored dogs tend to have more coat, they require a different sort of brush, which should be a *very soft* pin brush. Most pin brushes are too harsh for the Papillon as they might scratch the skin since there is no undercoat. No matter what kind of brush you buy and use, remember that all brushing is done gently.

Establish a grooming routine with your Papillon right from the beginning. If she is an older or a rescue dog, you will have to know what her grooming experience has been because you will have to adapt your grooming process to help the dog transition from her old life to her new, wonderful life with you. This should be done on the day you bring your Papillon home.

Getting started: To let your Papillon know that you are in charge of grooming, put her on the grooming table where you can talk reassuringly to her, scratch her behind the ears, and stroke her softly until you can feel her relax and begin to trust you. When you think she is relaxed, gently look at her teeth, check out her nails, and stroke her ears between your fingertips so that she will become accustomed to having you work with her ears for cleaning, bathing, and grooming.

After this activity, a small treat would be appropriate. However, treats should be given only after she has behaved properly and calmly. Go through this mock grooming routine at least daily for two weeks. Always make it a pleasant experience for her. When she seems to take the routine for granted, you can lessen the frequency gradually to approach the time, place, and frequency of the grooming sessions you plan to establish for her lifetime—probably twice a week.

Papillon Coat Care

The specifications for a proper Papillon coat, as stated in the breed standard, are there so that breeders will continue to work toward the ideal coat that is single, silky, and flowing. When your Papillon matures, her ear fringes will be of medium length. There are some mature dogs whose ear fringes are excessive and overdone, covering the front opening of the ear. This masks the flowing hair behind each ear, which represents the tail of the butterfly, and interferes with the overall butterfly impression. These excessive fringes are called *curtain fringes* and are more commonly found on dogs with the incorrect double coat (the silky coat with an undercoat).

A flowing coat, as mentioned in the standard, is a coat that moves when the dog moves. The coat does not fly around, it simply flows, with the movement of the dog. If the coat flows, it indicates that the texture and nature of the coat (single coated) are correct. This is the kind of coat you will welcome for its wash-and-wear quality.

Brushing: Since you have accustomed your Papillon to being on the grooming table, you must now teach her to lie quietly on her side while you brush her main coat. Before you begin, you must have your spray bottle filled with pure or bottled water. Test the spray to be sure that it is a very fine mist. Do not spray directly onto the coat. Wave the spray over the dog, holding the spray bottle above her at about arm's length. The Papillon's coat will brush more easily and preserve better if it is very slightly damp when you do your brushing. As you brush, be sure to comb through the coat and ear fringes.

One popular approach to brushing starts with the dog on her side. By starting at her tummy and using your brush, gently brush a line of hair down toward you. You will do this line brushing working your way up toward the spine. At each line you will need to do a misting of the hair before you brush. When you have reached the spine, turn her over and repeat the process on the other side. This will take care of the main body coat. Before you move to the chest hair, be sure you have gotten into one of the tough places—under the front legs (the underarm). Knots of hair tend to appear here, so do not let them start. The tail plume and the breeches can be separated into sections, misted, and gently brushed. Comb again, watching for knots.

Now she may sit up or you might want to teach her to lie down with her tummy flat on the table (like a sphinx). You must mist and brush the neck all around, including behind the ears. This is another place to watch for those

The Coat

The standard for the breed specifies the type, placement, and texture of the Papillon coat. In part, the standard states:

"Coat—Abundant, long, fine, silky, flowing, straight with resilient quality, flat on back and sides of body. A profuse frill on chest. There is no undercoat. Hair short and close on skull, muzzle, front of forelegs, and from hind feet to hocks. Ears well fringed, with the inside covered with silken hair of medium length. Backs of the forelegs are covered with feathers diminishing to the pasterns. Hind legs are covered to the hocks with abundant breeches (culottes). Tail is covered with a long, flowing plume. Hair on feet is short, but fine tufts may appear over toes and grow beyond them, forming a point."

knots of hair. The hair here must be kept free of knots because this hair is the tail of the butterfly. With one hand behind the ear to brace it, gently mist and brush the ear fringes. This is a good time to check the nails and do the teeth, but more about that later.

Bathing: All you will need for the Papillon bath is a good tearless baby shampoo, a quality brand name conditioner for normal hair, and a sink with a sprayer hose. Perfumed products are not desirable. If you do not have a sprayer hose, you will have to use a plastic container to pour water through the coat. If you are doing it this way, be absolutely sure that you have rinsed and rinsed again to get all of the soap out of the coat.

Put a rubber mat into the sink. While being very careful to keep water, shampoo, and conditioner out of her eyes and ears, start with the head and wet the coat and ear fringes. Apply

shampoo and squeeze the suds through the coat as you would when washing a wool sweater. Rinse, rinse, rinse. If necessary, although unusual, a second shampooing might be used. Once again, rinse, rinse, rinse. Now you will apply the conditioner in much the same way as the shampoo, being sure you pour the liquid through the ear fringes. Let the conditioner stay in the hair for a few minutes and then rinse, rinse, rinse. Do not condition a second time.

With clean towels blot the coat thoroughly, and you are almost finished. Let her have a good shake, and then the coat can drip-dry. It is not recommended but if you insist on using a handheld hair dryer, be absolutely sure the settings are on *low* heat and *low* air. Never put your Papillon into a crate with a dryer blowing into the crate. There is no way for her to escape if the crate is becoming overheated. There is also the danger of her being burned if she lies down with her body up against the dryer.

When she is completely dry, you can go on to the finishing touches. With your scissors, trim the hair between the pads of the feet. Then shape the hair around the feet to a point in the front, which enhances the hare foot of the Papillon. Whiskers on the Papillon may be trimmed off or left on. It is your choice. If you are going to trim them off, use your scissors, not clippers. Under the tail your scissors can be used to clean up, shorten, or neaten the hairs just around the anus. You are finished, and it is time for her to have a bathroom break, a little romp, and a treat.

Even this young puppy is sitting bravely for his grooming session. The time taken in reassuring your pet on the table will be a worthwhile investment.

Even though this Papillon is sitting politely to have his nails trimmed, he wants you to know that he doesn't have to like it! Notice the toys that are there to be used as distractions.

Doing the Dreaded Nails

If you keep your Papillon's nails trimmed properly, you should never hear them go click-clack on the kitchen floor. If you hear that sound, the nails have been neglected, could snag on fabrics or rugs, and could hurt and bleed a lot if a nail is torn off.

At least twice a month, you will want to trim her toenails. If you have any hesitation about doing this yourself, most professional grooming salons will take care of it for you for a small fee. Be sure to call ahead to make an appointment.

If you are going to do the nails yourself, this is one circumstance in which the early training will help. She will be used to having her feet touched and is not as likely to be resistant. Nails must be kept as short and blunt as possible, which is a chore with Papillons because they are seldom running around on cement where their activity would keep the nails worn down naturally. You should learn from an experienced person about nail trimming before you attempt this delicate grooming requirement. Once you have acquired the skill, you should not have any problems. Dewclaws (an extra nail) are usually removed on the Papillon, so that should not be a concern.

Cut the hollow tip of the nail to avoid injury to the sensitive quick. Since a Papillon's nails are clear, the quick is easy to see.

Holding her up in one arm while you work with the other is the best way to go about the trimming. Hold the paw in one hand, spreading the toes out so that you can quickly come in with the other hand for the trimming. This maneuver will take some practice. If you get a lot of resistance from her, wrap her body in a towel, exposing her head and, one by one, the foot on which you are going to work.

The dog's nail is made up of a hard outer shell that is the actual nail. Inside this is softer material with a vein running through it that is

called the quick. If you push back under your own fingernail until it hurts, you have gotten to the quick. Look at the underside of the dog's nails. The quick can be seen as the lighter center part within the circle of the nail. To shorten the nails, you must remove the pointed portion of the hard nail itself. Tip the nail with the clipper tip pointing at a backward slant toward the dog's body (\) instead of straight up and down. What you cut should be sort of crunchy. You must avoid cutting the quick. If the clipper goes through like butter you are too close to the quick. Removing just a tiny tip of the nail and trimming again soon is better than taking the chance of cutting the quick. If you do cut into the quick, it will hurt your Papillon and the nail will bleed a lot. Some styptic products on the market will stop this bleeding. However, if you do not have anything like that, you can try using flour or alum that you might have on hand in your kitchen. Put some of the material in the cup of your hand and press the bleeding nail into it until the bleeding stops. If she will not hold still for this, just put her into the sink and run cold water on the foot and nail until the bleeding stops and the blood clots.

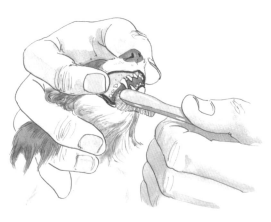

Cleaning Those Beautiful Butterfly Wings

A regular part of ear care is cleaning them. Cleaning can be done with a soft, dry cotton cloth on the end of your finger. The inside surface of the ear must be wiped very carefully and without injuring the ear canal. Never put a cotton swab down into the ear canal—there is too much potential danger to the eardrum.

No matter which type of ear your Papillon has, remember that healthy ears do not have a nasty smell. After all, what you want is a clean, sweet-smelling, and glamorous lap sitter.

Is Dental Care Really Necessary?

According to veterinary authorities, good dental health contributes to overall canine health. Plaque and tartar seem to build up more in smaller breeds, so dental care is a concern for Papillon owners. The bacteria that cause tooth and gum deterioration can travel through the bloodstream and damage other organs such as the heart and kidneys. Without proper care, tooth loss and gum disease are common for Papillons.

Preventive care: Put your Papillon on a routine of preventive dental care. Start by running your finger along the gum line and on the outside of her teeth. When she is used to this kind of exam, put a little pet toothpaste onto your finger and rub that onto her gums and teeth. Pet toothpaste is meat flavored so most dogs like it. Be sure to avoid human toothpastes as

When a dog is accustomed to having its mouth and teeth handled from early puppyhood, a program of effective oral hygiene becomes a routine part of its maintenance.

they contain too much fluoride and the foaming agents may cause vomiting. Never use a hand scaler or other instruments.

Use a toothbrush with soft bristles that have rounded ends. Start by brushing the outside of the front teeth in an up-and-down motion. Gradually extend your brushing back along the sides of the mouth until all teeth are brushed inside and out without resistance from your pet. After brushing, a small treat can reinforce that brushing is a positive event. If you have trouble getting her used to a toothbrush, just rub the teeth up and down with a moistened cloth with a bit of her toothpaste on it.

Tartar: If your girl builds too much tartar in spite of your daily care, she may have to have an occasional thorough cleaning, to be done under anesthetic by your veterinarian. Any time she has really bad breath, it could be indicative of serious systemic problems. If you notice this (and you will), consult your veterinarian immediately.

A common problem in toy breeds is that baby teeth often refuse to fall out or be pushed out by the incoming mature teeth. If the baby teeth are not loose and do not appear as though they are going to fall out, your veterinarian will have to pull them. Do not even think of doing this yourself. If the teeth are not loose, the roots are firmly in place; pulling them will have to be done under anesthetic or a heavy tranquilizer. Unless you plan to show her, you can have extra teeth pulled at the same time she is spayed.

Exercise

Exercise is never a problem with Papillons. They will exercise you quite efficiently. Papillons have their own built-in fitness regimen. Running, jumping, and bouncing up and down on their hind feet are all part of their regular activities. Because of their natural inclination to be active, you will not need to get up at early hours to take your dog for a run. This is another benefit of owning a Papillon.

Do not be too complacent. She will not allow you to become a couch potato. She will lure and entice you into the daily activities she has designed for you, which will include lots of playing.

Walking: This is better than running as exercise for you and for your Papillon. Walking will take you both out of the house, and she will have a chance to explore new sights, smells, sounds, and things. Make an effort to walk on soft surfaces like grass. Other surfaces may be too hot or tough for a house dog's pads. If you live in a snowy area, be careful not to walk your Papillon on salted roadways, as the salt can burn her pads. You might want to get her some doggy boots to wear to avoid this problem.

Swimming: Being around water can be very dangerous for your Papillon. Small dogs do not swim well for long. If you have a pool or you and the dog are going to be near water on a regular basis, you must teach her to swim. The steps in most pools are steep for a Papillon. The best thing to do is install a ramp and teach her how to get out of the pool using it. Never leave your Papillon near open water without close supervision.

Fetch: This is a favorite activity of the Papillon. She will retrieve balls, small disks, and any kind of toys or objects you throw for her. The Papillon never seems to tire. You will want to teach your Papillon that you will be the one to end the game and how you will do it.

Toys

What can be more fun than shopping for new toys for your puppy? Dog toys are everywhere, including in your supermarket. Many dog toys are attractive to a Papillon, but the really fun things for her are in the cat toy department. Cat toys are a better fit for her, but do not give her toys that contain catnip.

One of the really popular toys is the kind that has a feather or a group of feathers on the end of a flexible stick. All you have to do is hold the end of the stick and make the feather bob up and down. By doing so, you can entertain your Papillon for much longer than you imagined.

No matter whether you choose a dog toy or a cat toy, be very careful that the size of the toy is such that it will not get stuck in her throat and choke her. Always avoid small, smooth rubber balls that tend to get slimy and might slip down her throat. Never buy hard-plastic toys that might splinter. Latex, rubber, cotton rope, and

rawhide toys may come apart and pose a risk for her breathing or digestive system.

Chew sticks are all right for Papillons. They provide good exercise for the teeth and gums. They are useful to distract the dog away from chewing on things that are not allowed. They can keep the dog entertained when she has to be left alone and will keep her from becoming bored and barking. Tofu sticks are available if you have a concern about the way the hide in regular chew sticks is treated.

Travel Can Be Fun

If you plan to do a lot of travel, get your Papillon accustomed to being in a soft-sided tote bag that is designed especially for dogs. These are available from your pet supplier. If she is used to her bag, she can go on airplanes with you (under the seat) and into most situations where larger, uncontained dogs are not allowed (taxis, hotel rooms, and in some locations, restaurants).

When traveling, water of different qualities can cause all kinds of digestive problems for dogs. So you must have bottled water on hand for her. Make your Papillon a good companion and she will be welcome wherever you go in your travels.

Caution! Never leave your Papillon in a parked car, even if it is in the shade and the windows are cracked open. Within a few minutes on a warm day, the temperature inside the car can soar past 150°F (65°C). Your pet can die rapidly of heatstroke.

Puppy size toys are especially attractive for your Papillon youngster. He will choose his favorite of the moment.

Three examples of crates illustrate the fiberglass and wire crates and one of many types of soft-sided travel bags. All of the dogs appear to be very comfortable being in their enclosures.

CHECKLIST

Travel

✔ Be sure your Papillon is comfortable in her crate or travel bag.

✔ Get a health certificate from your veterinarian, including an up-to-date vaccination record.

✔ Gather any medications your pet will need on the trip.

✔ Make advanced reservations with hotels or campgrounds.

✔ Reserve space for your pet on the airline if you plan to keep her in the cabin with you.

✔ Be sure you have emergency items for your pet, including veterinary records and a photo ID.

✔ Have a good supply of materials to clean up after your pet (towels, plastic bags).

Successful training means consistency with one person doing the training. Papillons want to learn and please, so teaching basic manners can begin at once. Basic training includes good manners on leash, and obedience to "come," "sit, " "stay," and down commands.

Puppy training classes for younger, *inoculated,* puppies provide supervised socialization and training help for you. Your Papillon's breeder, your veterinarian, the yellow pages, and local newspaper can direct you to a trainer.

Useful Training Aids

When training, your Papillon should wear a flat, plain-buckle collar, loose enough to fit one finger between the collar and the dog's neck. You will need a 5-foot-long (1.5-m) lightweight cloth leash. Always have treats available.

Leash Training

For basic training, your Papillon should be comfortable on leash. Introduce her to walking with you on leash by holding the leash and letting her lead you. Then, call her to you. As you take a few steps,

coax her to come closer. When she comes to you, offer a treat and praise. Then end the session with a favorite game.

Never drag her to you on leash. This just increases her resistance. Gradually increase the distances she comes with you. Continue until coming with you is routine. If she gets sidetracked, stop, talk to her encouragingly, using her name. When she returns to you, give her a treat and continue walking for a short distance. End the session with a treat.

When she walks with you reliably, she is ready for formal heeling. By now she will be excited to see her leash and walk with you.

Come When Called

If you have used your Papillon's name from the moment you brought her home, getting her attention will be easy. Call her name, encouraging her to you for meals. She will make a positive association with coming to you. For fun activities, call her name, coaxing her to you. Offer treats at first; when she responds to her name, decrease the number of times you treat. Give treats randomly, but praise always. Praise will soon get your Papillon to do whatever you ask.

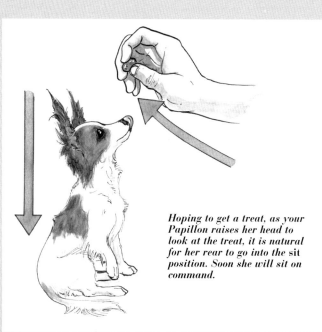

Hoping to get a treat, as your Papillon raises her head to look at the treat, it is natural for her rear to go into the sit *position. Soon she will sit on command.*

Sit on Command

With your Papillon on your left, command, *"Sit."* At the same time, let her see and smell a treat in front of her nose; move the treat upward, holding it just above her head. She will have to look up and back to see the treat. Her head will rise and it will be more natural for her rear to go down, but you may have to guide her into the sit. When she sits, praise *("Good Sit")* and treat. Do not expect her to sit on command until you have practiced this several times. When she sits on command unguided, give her treats and ample praise.

As with coming when called, gradually decrease the frequency of treats after she sits on command. Soon praise alone will be enough reward.

After your Papillon has learned to sit on command, you can teach her to lie down by holding a treat close to the floor and in front of her. As you move the treat out in front of her, she should naturally go into a down position as she follows the treat with her nose.

Down on Command

Be sure your Papillon is confident about her *sit* before teaching the *down* command. From grooming your Papillon on a table, you already have her lying down during grooming sessions. Now teach her to lie down on command. With her on a *sit,* hold a treat in front of her, near the floor. Starting from between her front legs, slowly move the treat out in front of her while commanding *"Down."* She should assume a *down* position from following the treat with her nose. If she needs help at first, very gentle pressure on her shoulders should get her into the *down* position. When she is down, treat and praise her.

Continue practicing until she lies down on command. Gradually put the treat farther in front of her, keeping it near the ground. Make her hold the *down* as you praise and treat her and until you release her with an *"OK."*

Stay on Command

Getting your Papillon to stay in one place can be a challenge. One way to accomplish this is to have her sit on a step about 2 to 4 inches (5 to 10 cm) above the ground or floor. Give the *stay* command, showing her your flat palm. At first stay about 6 inches (15 cm) from the step, but right in front of the dog. She will probably try to join you. When she moves from the *sit,* put her back gently, saying *"Stay."* When she stays for even an instant, praise and treat her. As she stays in place, gradually increase your distance from her and the length of time between the *stay* command, her response, and reward. Use small increments and repeat each level until she is steady and comfortable in her behavior at that level.

FEEDING YOUR PAPILLON

The health, longevity, and beauty of our dogs start from the inside and depend in part on a nutritious, well-balanced diet. Papillons have some special dietary needs, and it is up to you to provide for those needs.

Starting Off Right

On the path to domestication, canine ancestors were lucky to have some meat and bone leftovers in the homes of cavepeople. Dogs in those times were omnivorous. They ate everything, including meat, vegetables, and roughage (brush and grasses). Their diet was fairly well balanced. By the laws of survival, those who did not find enough good nutrition died. In contrast, the tough or clever ones survived. As dogs became closer companions of humans, they became more dependent on people for their care and survival. It remains our responsibility to provide healthful nutrition for our dogs from puppyhood through geriatrics.

Whether you are getting a puppy from a breeder, an adult dog, or a rescue dog, it is critical that you continue for at least two weeks to feed the same diet to which the dog is accustomed. If any changes in diet are

Here's a young Papillon in good condition. Proper feeding and exercising to keep him in that condition is up to you.

necessary, you should introduce new items gradually over about ten days to avoid any major stomach or intestinal upsets.

Dietary Needs Change

All throughout the Papillon's life, his dietary needs will vary according to his level of activity. Running around the house is not the same level of activity as that of a field dog that is running outside through brush to find or retrieve game. If you and your Papillon become involved in obedience, agility, or fun doggy team sports, the amount of food will have to be increased to compensate for the increased activity.

It is very important for your Papillon puppy that he has at least four small meals a day (see "How Much to Feed and When"). This schedule helps to maintain his blood sugar at a healthy level. The diet of the younger dog will be richer in nutrients to provide for growth and development. As he matures to young adulthood, meals can be decreased gradually until he is at a lifetime schedule of two meals per day.

Older Papillons will need to be fed twice a day, although those meals will have to be smaller so that the less active dog will not become obese.

Other Things Affecting Diet

It is not likely that any Papillon will spend much time outdoors alone or in a kennel. That is not the kind of life that is right for a Papillon. Modifying the diet to accommodate changes in the weather will not be necessary.

In some lines or families, dogs can tend to be overweight or underweight no matter how carefully the dog's diet is managed. Genetics can influence the Papillon's needs for different calorie levels, the ways in which the dog metabolizes foods, and problems with digestion. All of these problems are specific to individual dogs. If you suspect a dietary or nutritional problem, consult with your veterinarian for possible testing and dietary review.

Alternative Diets

An increasing number of Papillon breeders have been feeding their dogs fresh food that has been living recently or has been fresh frozen. The basis of these diets is raw, organically produced, high-grade protein ranging from chicken to kangaroo. Added to this are cooked organic vegetables and appropriate carbohydrates. Some breeders prepare their own food. However, prepared foods are available, some of which come frozen for later use (see "Information"). The most controversial element of this diet is the feeding of *uncooked* bones.

Positive reports by users seem to offset fears of feeding the raw diet if safe food-handling procedures are used. Arguments that the raw food diet increases the risk of choking, intestinal blockage, or contracting salmonella or *Escherichia coli* are not substantiated by proponents of this diet. Papillon breeders who use this raw diet report improvement in the amount and quality of coat, the condition of the teeth, and the size and viability of litters. Instead of having one-puppy litters by Caesarean section, the raw diet is credited with four- and five-puppy litters whelped naturally. Papillon breeders also proclaim that the raw foods diet boosts the immune system, resulting in fewer allergies and better overall health.

These alternative diets are not endorsed here any more than are the conventional commercial diets. This material is provided for information.

Interpreting Commercial Dog Food Labels

Most major dog food manufacturers have spent millions of dollars in research to develop canned and dry foods that their research indicates are nutritious and healthy for dogs. These companies conduct quality control programs to assure the continued balance of their food formulas. Manufacturers will list different amounts of information on their labels regarding their product. All dog foods are required by the American Association of Food Control Officials (AAFCO) to contain similar percentages of organic components that are required to meet a dog's daily nutritional allowance. The AAFCO also requires that dog food labels must have a statement about the nutritional adequacy of the product (for example, "complete and balanced nutrition"). These certifications may be measured through laboratory or feeding tests or they may be calculated using a standard table of ingredients called the AAFCO nutrient profile.

Analysis

Every label will include a guaranteed analysis that lists the minimum percentages of protein and fat and the maximum percentages of fiber and moisture contained in the product. A few basic ingredients are essential in dog food: protein, carbohydrates, fats, vitamins and minerals, and water. A list on the label will include all the components in the product that make up the percentages claimed in the analysis. Ingredients are listed in decreasing order (by weight) and will include food additives, artificial colorings and flavorings, and food preservatives, if any. This general information does not tell you the quality of the sources of ingredients nor does it tell you anything about nutrient availability or digestibility.

Protein quality is the most important health factor in a dog's diet. Dog foods that contain grains may cause allergic reactions such as hot spots (eczema-like spots along with loss of hair). Common protein sources found in dog foods include beef, chicken, lamb, fish, and eggs. The way in which these proteins are included is important. If they are meat by-products, they might include lungs, spleen, kidneys, brain, livers, blood, bone fatty tissue, and stomachs and intestines freed of their contents. If they are poultry by-products, they may include heads, feet, and viscera free from fecal content and foreign matter except in trace amounts.

If the food contains by-products, that means head, feet, and other lesser-quality protein. If it contains meal, it means that the protein source has been ground to particles. By-products and meal may be a less expensive protein source for the manufacturer, but they are poor quality sources for a Papillon's nutrition. Papillons need extra digestible protein from high-quality animal sources, which provide a good amino acid balance for dogs. This same kind of protein cannot be obtained from grains or plant sources.

Commercial foods are designed for average dogs, not for individuals. Papillons do not have a genetic predisposition to dietary-caused anomalies, but they do not have the same requirements as a Great Dane. A premium brand of commercial food will not meet the needs of every dog anymore than a homemade diet will. You may have to experiment to find which diet suits your Papillon best.

TIP

Caution!

Never, ever give your Papillon a cooked bone. Cooked bones are dangerous. They are brittle from being cooked and can splinter, causing life-threatening damage to the Papillon's digestive or intestinal system.

If you and your Papillon are running agility courses every day and doing fly-ball for a hobby, the percentage of protein in his diet may have to be increased. If the added protein is too much, your Papillon's normal activity level might increase to a degree that is not comfortable for you or for him, which means he is having to work harder to use the added calories. Balance is the important idea. Find the right balance in his daily food needs and keep it there.

Fats are important ingredients in the dog's diet, adding to the flavor and enhancing skin and coat condition. Fats also help digestion and provide energy. They are required for the assimilation of the fat-soluble vitamins A, D, E, and K. Different fats have different effects on the body. Veterinarians believe that dogs benefit most from fats that are liquid at room temperature, such as vegetable and fish oils.

Carbohydrates: Even though we do not yet know whether or how much dogs might need carbohydrates, they make up a major portion of commercial dog foods because they are cheap. They usually come in the form of corn, corn meal, rice, or some combination of grains. Dogs do not digest fiber well, and some dogs may have an intestinal reaction to this kind of dry bulk. Fibers are useful in weight-reduction diets, which would indicate that they are not of good nutritional quality in maintaining an ideal weight.

Vitamins and minerals: Appropriate levels of these supplements need to be a daily part of the Papillon's diet. Vitamins A, D, E, and K are fat-soluble vitamins, and they are needed only in the prescribed amounts. Overdoing any of these fat-soluble vitamins can be very dangerous, as they store up from day to day in the dog's system and can be toxic or fatal. The water-soluble vitamins are C and all of the B vitamins. Dogs manufacture their own vitamin C (unlike humans) and do not need any supplement of this vitamin. The B vitamins do not store in the system and will not become toxic at high levels. In fact, if your Papillon is under stress, such as teething, being in season, or being shown in competitions, increased doses of multi-B vitamins can relieve the effects of the stress.

Most dog foods include the minerals calcium, phosphorus, sodium, potassium, magnesium, zinc, selenium, iron, manganese, copper, or iodine in some form or combination. Like vitamins, minerals must be given in a healthy balance in your pet's diet.

Well-balanced commercial vitamin/mineral supplements are available in your pet store, at a health food store, or from your veterinarian. When used as prescribed on the label, these balanced supplements can be beneficial and convenient. They are safer than mixes you might make on your own because a balanced measure of ingredients is guaranteed by the manufacturer.

Additives and preservatives: Different substances are added to commercial dog food to enhance color and flavor or to prevent fats in the food from becoming rancid. In this way, the products have a longer shelf life. Other additives may be used to delay bacterial and fungal growth. Unless you are a nutritionist or a chemist, the substances that are listed will have little meaning for you. A translation may be obtained from the AAFCO.

Food Allergies

Papillons can develop allergies to the contents of certain foods. Some dogs are sensitive to the kinds of carbohydrates that are contained in commercial dog foods. Other ingredients, such

No matter what age, a Papillon's health starts from within. The nutritional quality of his diet will be reflected in his coat, eyes, activity, and general condition.

as the oil or meat proteins, can also cause sensitivities. These allergies are expressed most often by effects on the skin, in the coat, or in the digestive system. Even so-called hypoallergenic diets may result in digestive upsets for a Papillon. The first signs of allergies may include excessive scratching or persistent loose stools. Consult with your veterinarian for possible dietary changes.

How Much to Feed and When

Nutritional needs will vary according to the stage of development, activity level, and environment. Most Papillon breeders like to have puppies gain about 1 pound (0.5 kg) per month from birth up to about age six months, at which point their growth and weight should stabilize. Adults should maintain a weight that is in good balance with their size and proportion. An adult, 5-pound (2.3 kg) Papillon might eat only 0.3 to 0.5 cups (80 to 140 mL) of high-quality food per day. It seems like a small amount, but remember that the breed standard says that the Papillon is "small, elegant and of fine-boned structure."

Being sure that your dog does not lose weight is just as important as being sure that he is not gaining too much too fast. Do not be fooled by the coat. A fluffy coat may make your Papillon appear heavier than he is. When you groom him, you will be able to feel his body to get an idea of his condition. Adjusting the amount of food given in each meal can

add or subtract weight quickly in a Papillon. Check your Papillon's weight once a week. Weigh yourself. Pick up your Papillon, and note your combined weight. Subtract your weight from the combined weight, and you will have a good measure of his weight. If you prefer, ask your veterinarian to weigh him.

Feeding Time

Everyone in the household must follow the same rules regarding the Papillon's care and feeding. Go over the rules with family members to be sure everyone understands them. If someone is overfeeding or giving treats or scraps from the table, you will end up with a finicky eater who is probably overweight.

No begging allowed: Do not allow your Papillon loose in the kitchen while you are preparing human meals or near the table when humans are eating. These are danger zones, where it is all too easy to give him just a little bit. A good procedure is to feed him first and have him in his crate or special place before humans are about to eat. Prevention can avoid having a begging dog. Much later he can be

TIP

Crate Feeding

Many Papillon owners feed their dogs in their crates. If you have more than one pet, feeding them in their crates is an excellent way of monitoring how much each one is eating and whether each one is eating his or her allocated supplements.

taught to beg for treats, but that should be in connection with the trick of sitting up and should never take place in the kitchen or dining room. If he tries to do this trick in the danger zones, make an ugly *"Aaaack"* sound, shake your index finger, and use a *"No beg"* command to stop that behavior.

Feeding schedules: Mealtimes should be on a regular schedule at the same times each day. Your Papillon will let you know the time of day when his internal dinner bell goes off. He will increase his activity level, go to his eating area, bring you a series of toys, or jump into your lap and give you the "I'm starving" stare.

Bowls: Your Papillon should have his own bowls. The best bowls are stainless steel, which are easy to wash and can be put through the dishwasher on a routine basis. Some cute, ceramic bowls are also dishwasher safe. Be sure they are nonporous and do not contain lead. Have a designated place for food and water bowls.

Finicky eaters: Papillons might become finicky eaters if allowed. To entice a noneater, a nervous owner is inclined to try all sorts of exotic foods, even lobster or filet mignon.

The problem with those enticements is that they are not balanced foods and they do not work. The Papillon soon discovers that he can get extra attention and a few goodies if he just refuses to eat. Feeding becomes a power play. Even the goodies will be rejected after a few days. It is time to review basic mealtime rules.

Until he has good eating habits, one of the best rules of feeding is to allow your Papillon to eat only what is in his personal bowl. Everything he is to eat should be put into that bowl, including treats, which should be calculated as part of the daily diet. Whatever treats he gets should be compatible with his regular food. Do not use human snack foods as treats for your Papillon. Human foods often contain sugars and salts that can be just as harmful for a dog as they are for humans.

If you have a finicky Papillon, when you feed him stay around so that he will not go in search of you. If he moves away from his bowl and comes to you, do not acknowledge him or talk to him. Ignore him and hope that he will go back to his bowl. After ten minutes, no matter whether the meal is finished or not, pick up the bowl and throw the remainder away. Never refeed what has been left. After having to pick up an unfinished meal, do not offer any sort of food until the next meal is due, not even a treat. When the next mealtime comes, follow the same procedure. Very soon your Papillon will learn to eat all of his meal immediately, and being finicky will become a thing of the past.

Obesity

Obesity is a condition that is especially threatening for Papillons because they like food. One of the disorders common in Papillons is loose or weakened patellas (kneecaps). If the dog is overweight, this adds stress to the patellas. This is similar to the knee problems created in obese humans. If the patellas are slipping out of place on a regular basis, surgery may be required.

Overfeeding is not the only cause of obesity. Feeding too much fat in the dog's diet will cause malnutrition, which leads to obesity. For humans and for dogs, obesity has reached epidemic proportions in the United States. Obese humans are now having difficulty obtaining health insurance. Another parallel between humans and dogs is that obesity can lead to heart disease, arthritis, and diabetes. Prevention involves providing the correct diet and correct amounts of exercise.

Water

Your Papillon should have free access to fresh water at all times, even in the car. Nonspill and collapsible bowls that sit well on the floor of a vehicle are avilable. Dogs lose body water all day long through urine and feces, evaporation, panting, drooling, and sweating through their foot pads. Since a 10 percent loss of water will cause a dog's death, you can see how important it is to have water always available.

If the weather is hot or if you and your Papillon are out doing active things, he will lose water at a faster rate. In such a situation, you will probably carry a bottle of water for yourself. Share it with your companion.

A Papillon's intake of water can be an important indicator of possible medical problems. Drinking too much water might indicate diabetes or kidney disease, including a condition called diabetes insipidus, which involves a huge intake of water and a huge urine output. You would notice this because it would be hard for him to maintain his house-training. If he is not drinking enough water, he could become dehydrated and might develop bladder or kidney problems. This is especially dangerous for a Papillon since they are prone to developing bladder crystals or stones. If there is a change in your Papillon's normal drinking habits, a visit to the veterinarian is important.

Food Myths

No matter what "facts" you have heard or read, garlic does not prevent worms or kill fleas in dogs any more than it prevents vampires. Brewer's yeast has been credited as a flea repellent, but this has never been substantiated. Dogs can benefit from yeast tablets in other ways since yeast contains B vitamins. Yeast tablets make a good, healthy reward treat.

Another myth is that onions are flea repellents. Not only is that not true, onions can be toxic or deadly in dogs. Dogs should never be fed onions.

The safest way to deal with myths about what certain foods do to perform miracles in dogs is to forget them and stay with your Papillon's care and maintenance schedules.

TIP

Another Caution!
Curb any urges you might have to share your food or supplements with your Papillon. His nutritional needs are different from yours. Look at it this way: would you base your routine diet on his food?

KEEPING YOUR PAPILLON HEALTHY

Your Papillon's physical and emotional health will thrive if she is given proper preventive care. She will need regular visits with her veterinarian and regular attention from you. A Papillon should never appear depressed or disinterested in life. If you see those signs, a health checkup is needed.

How Your Papillon Gets Care

The best way to keep your Papillon healthy is to find a good veterinarian and establish a regular schedule of preventive care for her. At the first visit, she will have a physical examination, be checked for parasites, and receive her proper vaccinations. Prevention that you can provide includes correct nutrition, daily dental care, routine grooming, and regular exercise. Your loving attention is a serious component of your Papillon's well-being.

Your Papillon has come to you in good health and it is up to you and your veterinarian to see that this healthy condition is maintained throughout your pet's life.

Selecting a Veterinarian

Finding a veterinarian with whom you have a good relationship is like searching for a pediatrician for your child or a specialist for yourself. Papillons have very special needs, especially in regard to vaccinations and dental care. So your selection will have an important impact on your puppy's health and life.

Deciding on a veterinarian before you bring your Papillon home is a good idea. Talk to your Papillon's breeder or the other Papillon lovers you have found, and ask for their recommendations about veterinarians. Their experience will be very helpful.

Checklist for Selecting a Veterinarian

Check out the office hours and their availability on weekends and holidays or in an emergency.

Look for a clinic that is close to your home.

Stop by the clinic and have a chat with the front office personnel.

Do they seem to know anything about Papillons?

Are the veterinary technicians fully trained (certified or licensed)?

How much responsibility do the technicians have for the care of the animals?

Ask about fees for services and what forms of payment are acceptable.

Set up an appointment to meet the veterinarian and have a tour of the facility.

Ask where the veterinarian received his or her degrees.

Check for cleanliness and absence of offensive odors.

If you are comfortable with the veterinarian, your search has ended.

Preventive Health Care

You are the one who spends the most time with your Papillon. You have the opportunity to check for any apparent problems with her eyes, ears, teeth, or coat when you are grooming her. It is also a time that you check her body for proper weight. Here are some signs of trouble that may help you decide whether you need to contact the veterinarian.

Check for fever before you call: Taking the temperature is not too difficult, using a digital rectal thermometer. Lubricate the tip of the thermometer with petroleum jelly and gently insert it about 1.5 inches (4 cm) into her rectum. Hold it in place, and do not let her sit on it. After two minutes (or if the thermometer signals it is ready), remove it and note her temperature. A dog's normal temperature range is from 99.5 to 102.5°F (37.5 to 39.2°C). A slight elevation may just mean that she is excited. If her temperature is more than one full degree over 102.5°F (39.2°C), indicating a fever, or more than one full degree below 99.5°F (37.5°C), indicating possible shock, call your veterinarian.

The first things you are most likely to notice as out of the ordinary are vomiting or diarrhea. Dehydration is a definite danger. If these signs are persistent, take the dog's temperature and call your veterinarian. Other signs of danger include difficulty breathing or swallowing, blood in the urine or stools, and problems with urinating or having bowel movements.

Circulatory problems: Papillons are subject to a number of circulatory problems, most notably high degrees of congenital heart problems, congestive heart failure, and heart murmur. Signs you might notice include a persistent cough that is deep in the chest, and the absence of an elevated temperature. That cough should be enough to precipitate a visit to the veterinarian.

Persistent sneezing (in which the dog bounces her nose on the floor with each sneeze) might indicate a foreign object up the dog's nose. Reverse sneezing (repeatedly sucking air back into the nose with vigor) occurs with some frequency in Papillons. There is a possible relationship between reverse sneezing and an elongated soft palate, but reports of this are anecdotal. The dogs that tend to reverse sneeze will do it when they are suddenly excited or when they are on a tight lead. Some people calm the behavior by holding the dog's nose and stroking her throat. Some dogs can be distracted from the behavior by being given a treat.

Limping and pain: If your Papillon is limping or showing signs of pain (crying out when she moves or when you touch her), she will need an examination by her veterinarian. Remember that Papillons have a high incidence of patellar luxation (loose kneecaps), especially if they are obese. If a kneecap has popped out of its normal location, this often causes a temporary hitch in the dog's movement in which the dog will hold the affected leg up or hop on the other three feet. Sometimes the patella will pop back into place on its own. Doing this manually is usually easy. However, if the condition is persistent, surgery may be needed.

You can deal with choking, but it must be done as quickly as possible. Be sure you have removed the cause of choking and, if necessary, take the dog to the veterinarian for follow-up.

Regular eye checks: A Papillon's eyes should be bright and clear of any hazy or cloudy condition. The whites should not show inflammation, and no mucus should be inside the bottom eyelid or in the corner of the eye. Many Papillons have a tear discharge that stains and discolors the area beneath the eye. This is sometimes treated internally with antibiotics and externally with a mild solution of boric acid. Commercial eye wipes are available at your pet store that may help with this external cleansing.

According to a 2000 survey conducted by the Papillon Club of America, Papillons are prone to considerable problems with cataracts, some juvenile but prodominantly senile type.

Regular ear checks: If you smell a bad odor near the ears, there may be an infection that needs treatment by the veterinarian.

Habitual head shaking can mean severe ear problems. Every time you comb your Papillon's ear fringes, look at the inside of the ears for any dark, smelly buildup. This exudate, combined with head shaking, may be a sign of ear mites (tiny critters whose eggs are more visible as small white particles that stick to the ear hair). Commercial and veterinary remedies for ear mites are easy to use and are very effective.

Regular dental checks. Proper dental care is discussed in the chapter "At Home with Your Papillon." Daily brushing is a definite requirement.

Regular coat checks: One of your Papillon's greatest attributes is her beautiful single, shiny coat. When dogs are not feeling well or if their nutrition is off balance, the effects may show up in the appearance of the coat. Excessive shedding may occur, and the coat may look dull and lifeless. As you go through the coat, look for any eczema spots, fleas, ticks, or other parasites. Remedies for these conditions exist and are available from your veterinarian or commercial sources.

Other checks: Papillons are prone to umbilical hernias (bulging, severe outies at the belly button), which are hereditary. Hernias can be corrected surgically to close the opening and this prevents more serious extrusion problems from developing later.

A condition similar to a hernia is a failure of the skull to close completely, leaving a soft spot on top of the head called a fontanel or molera. No treatment is available for this condition.

Another area that needs to be checked is the dog's rear end. If your female has not been spayed yet, she will have to be watched carefully so that she does not get bred accidentally. A visual check under the tail can catch problems such as swelling, cysts, inflammation, and tapeworms. If you have a male Papillon that has not been neutered, he must be checked

for undescended testicles. Since this is a common problem in Papillons and can lead to cancer later in life, neutering is in order.

Vaccinations

Vaccinations against serious, life-threatening diseases are given to most puppies on a regular schedule that has been worked out by expert immunologists in veterinary medicine. This schedule calls for vaccinations against distemper, hepatitis, parvovirus, and parainfluenza at eight weeks of age with subsequent follow-up vaccinations as determined necessary, usually up to 16 weeks. Other vaccinations for leptospirosis, bordetella, and rabies are scheduled for later administration. In geographical areas where Lyme disease is endemic, immunizations against that disease are scheduled on an as needed basis.

Everything about this young Papillon gives the impression of good health. Not only is he physically fit, he is out and about and ready to sail!

Because Papillons have weak immune systems, they are very sensitive to vaccines. The customary schedules of injection may not be right for your puppy. Most toy dogs have a greater risk of adverse reactions to vaccines. Vaccinations are a medical decision, and Papillons do not fit into the calendar that is published for the general canine population. Consult with your Papillon's breeder and your veterinarian to determine a recommended schedule of immunizations that is appropriate for your Papillon.

The common canine diseases, Lyme disease, bordetella, and leptospirosis, are spread bacterially through tick bites or contamination of the dog's food or water. Distemper, parvovirus, canine hepatitis, parainfluenza, and rabies are viral and are spread by airborne particles from sneezes and coughs, contaminated body excretions, or in the case of rabies, through saliva, most commonly in bite wounds. In order to be immune from rabies, which is fatal once symptoms occur, dogs must be inoculated before exposure. Immediate postexposure treatment via a series of simple shots is available for humans.

Parasite Control

There are internal parasites and external parasites. None of these is good for a Papillon's health. Some of them are transmittable to you. If signs of parasites are present, your veterinarian will prescribe proper medication to correct the condition.

Internal parasites: Quite early, probably on her first visit, the veterinarian will ask you to come back with a sample of your puppy's stool. The presence of internal parasites or their eggs is detected by examining the stool.

Roundworms used to be so common in dogs that all puppies were wormed routinely on the assumption that they had these worms, which can be passed along to puppies in the mother's uterus or in her milk. Proper cleanliness in the areas where dogs relieve themselves has helped to reduce the incidence of roundworms. Since accidental ingestion of eggs from contact with infected feces is the means by which these worms might be passed along to you, it is very important to wash your hands thoroughly after any possible contact with your dog's feces.

Tapeworms are passed along through fleas. Proper and regular flea control can prevent these worms from becoming established in

your puppy's system. Remember the Papillon's sensitivity to chemical substances such as malathion or other insecticides and be sure that any flea control sprays you use are non-toxic for dogs.

Hookworms are transmitted through contact with feces or direct skin contact with larvae in contaminated soil. These worms are more common in some parts of the country than others. If you live in an endemic area, you should not walk around outside in bare feet.

Heartworms are not transmitted to humans but can be deadly to dogs. Infection is caused by mosquito bite, so your dog should not be left out for long periods after dark when mosquitos are on the prowl, especially if you live near any body of still water where mosquitos might breed. If a blood test indicates your dog is not infected, she can be started on a safe program of preventive medication secured through her veterinarian.

The full, lustrous coat carried by this dog is a reliable indicator of good internal health. The likelihood of finding worms in this Papillon is little to none.

External parasites: Fleas, ticks, and sarcoptic mange cause serious health problems for dogs. Flea bites cause irritation and itching and can be the means of transmitting tapeworms. Tick bites also itch and can become infected. The bite of some ticks can transmit Lyme disease. Sarcoptic mange causes skin eruptions, itching, and hair loss and is contagious by contact to humans. Another form of mange, demodectic mange, affects only dogs, causes skin eruptions and hair loss, and is often passed from mother to puppies.

The Senior Papillon

If you have more than one pet, your elder Papillon will need a place and times that are safe from the intrusions of other pets or more active dogs. An extrasoft bed will help with any arthritis or joint problems. If your Papillon becomes hard of hearing or develops cataracts, be careful not to startle her when you wake her. A light touch should get her attention without scaring her.

Activities for the senior Papillon should be restricted to those that are comfortable for her. Easy, short walks are in order, and she should no longer be expected to climb stairs. Since she will be less active, her weight should be monitored so that she does not become obese. It is equally important to be sure she does not lose too much weight. Around the house it might be wise to teach her to use a ramp to get on and off beds, chairs, or sofas. Even in old age, Papillons think they can fly.

Trips to the veterinarian should be more frequent to watch for conditions that can be cured, prevented, or alleviated.

Euthanasia—Crossing the Rainbow Bridge

Euthanasia is the term for letting your beloved pet go humanely, peacefully, and painlessly. Even with the super care you have given her, the day will come when you must consider saying good-bye. This is one of the hardest decisions you will have to make. Imagining life without your Papillon is hard, but age or illness sometimes catches up and you are helpless to change that. You will not want her to suffer. If her pain cannot be relieved or if her quality of life is poor, with too many bad days, it is time to discuss the situation with your veterinarian, who will help you with your decision. If you decide that euthanasia is necessary, the most commonly used method is the administration of a sedative to relax her and make her sleep deeply, followed by the injection of a substance that deepens her sleep and ends her life instantly and painlessly. Your veterinarian can advise you about pet cemeteries and cremation services.

People who have never been owned by a dog find it easy to tell you that you should be happy you have another one (or more) at home to take your dear Papillon's place. They just do not understand that no dog can take her place. She had a lifetime of being herself in her own unique ways. You will need to be able to convert your grief to happy memories. You must allow yourself whatever grieving process you need. If you find your grief continuing at an uncomfortable level after a couple of months, consult a grief counselor or therapist who can help you with your sadness. Just remember that you took excellent care of your pet all through her life, and even though it was terribly difficult, your decision about her final comfort was in her best interests.

Diseases Common in Papillons

Circulatory problems	Heart problems, including murmurs and congestive heart failure, are reported at moderately high levels.
Digestive problems	Hardly any problems reported except a fairly low percentage with inability to gain weight.
Endocrine problems	Hypoglycemia (a sudden drop in blood sugar level) continues to be the foremost problem, especially in small or young dogs.
Ear and Eye problems	Senile cataracts are common. Progressive retinal atrophy (PRA) is found in Papillons.
Musculoskeletal problems	Patellar luxation is the most common problem, with at least 50 percent affected in one knee or both. Bone fractures, open fontanel/molera, inguinal hernia, cleft palate, and other deformities are reported at recognizable levels.
Neurological problems	Epilepsy, hydrocephalus, and slipped disk appear moderately.
Dental/periodontal problems	Tooth loss and extraction occur in more than 50 percent of adult dogs, despite tooth cleaning by a veterinarian. This may be from periodontal disease due to neglect of daily dental care.
Reproductive problems	False pregnancy, infertility, and spontaneous resorptions (fetuses resorbed by the female before they reach full term) occur.
Skin/hair problems	Allergies resulting in skin conditions occur in noticeable numbers.
Urological/genital problems	Nearly 40 percent of males have retained (undescended) testicles. Bladder stones or crystals, urinary tract infections, and kidney failure commonly occur.

If there are children in the family, talk to them about the loss of their pet at a level they can understand. Do not talk about "putting her to sleep," as this may trigger a fear in the children of going to sleep themselves. It is all right to say that it was time for your Papillon's life to end. Explain that her age and condition made it hard for her to enjoy her life. Give them whatever comfort they need, and let them share their grief with you.

Selected Diseases and Conditions

Once they grow up, Papillons are hardy and resilient. Like most breeds of dogs, Papillons can have conditions or disorders to which they are predisposed. This does not mean that your Papillon will ever experience any of those problems. The breeder or person from whom you got your Papillon should be able to tell you about the occurrence of any of these problems in her ancestors.

Don't let the Papillon's coat fool you. An abundance of coat can mask an underweight body or can make a fit body appear obese.

A Phalene, like any other drop-eared dog, may be more predisposed to ear infections than its erect-eared counterparts. Regular care and cleaning of ears will help avoid these problems.

Family history comes into play in your Papillon's health and condition. The family tree will give you an idea about how you might expect your pet to thrive.

Papillons, like dogs of all breeds, are predisposed to certain diseases and conditions. This does not mean, however, that your dog will experience such health problems during her lifetime. Ask the breeder about any health issues that may be prevalent in your dog's family.

When accidents happen, it will be up to you to do emergency procedures until you can get to your veterinarian's office or the emergency clinic. You should have a first aid kit on hand. Remember this is first aid for emergencies only.

After giving first aid, keep your Papillon as quiet as possible and get her to a veterinarian right away for treatment.

Emergency Numbers

National Animal Poison Control Center:
1-888-426-4435

Your veterinarian's phone number

Emergency veterinary clinic phone numbers

Handling the Injured Papillon

Remember, the Papillon is small and easy to handle. If she reacts to trauma with panic, place a small blanket or towel over her head before you pick her up. This will keep her from lashing out and biting you by accident.

Checklist for the First Aid Kit

✔ Nutri-Cal or honey to treat hypoglycemia
✔ Rectal thermometer
✔ Hydrogen peroxide 3 percent
✔ Opthalmic ointment
✔ Sterile gauze pads
✔ Roll of gauze bandage
✔ Paper towels
✔ Nontoxic antiseptic
✔ Small flashlight

✔ Instructions on doing CPR
✔ Antibacterial hand wipes
✔ Wood paint stirrer (splint)

Specific Emergencies

After you have given any form of first aid, get your Papillon to a veterinarian for treatment or a checkup.

Symptoms: shallow breathing, confusion, pale gums. Cause: shock. Action: wrap her in a warm blanket and get to the veterinarian.

Symptoms: coughing, gagging, pawing at mouth, shaking head. Cause: choking. Action: check mouth and throat for objects; remove objects.

Symptoms: bleeding profusely. Cause: open wound. Action: stop bleeding with pressure applied to sterile gauze pads over the wound.

Symptoms: minor bleeding. Cause: bite or puncture wound. Action: encourage bleeding and cleanse with clear running water.

Symptoms: whimpering, favoring a limb, or lying immobile. Cause: broken bone, dislocation, sprain. Action: wrap her and get to the nearest professional help.

Symptoms: red or blistered skin. Cause: burns. Action: do not treat; wrap in a clean cloth and get to professional help.

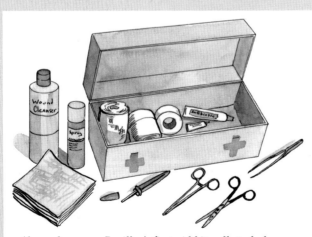

Always keep your Papillon's first aid kit well stocked. You never know when you will need it.

PAPILLON FIRST AID

Symptoms: panting excessively, breathing with difficulty. Cause: heatstroke. Action: get her into cool water or wrap her in wet towels; get immediate professional help.

Symptoms: unconscious in or around water. Cause: drowning. Action: hold your Papillon up by the hind legs to let water run out; conduct gentle artificial respiration and/or CPR.

Symptoms: retching, pain, trembling, convulsions, rigidity. Cause: poisoning from rodent bait, garbage, or antifreeze. Action: call your veterinarian or the poison hotline and get her to professional help; if she is rigid, do not try any first aid.

All garden or household chemicals should be kept well out of your Papillon's reach.

Symptoms: lid closed on inflamed or watery eye. Cause: scratches or foreign object in eye. Action: flush with water and apply ophthalmic ointment.

Symptoms: localized swelling. Cause: bee or wasp sting. Action: remove stinger and bathe the area with water or a solution of bicarbonate of soda in lukewarm water; apply first aid cream.

Symptoms: electric shock with shaking and rigidity. Cause: puppy chewing through electric cord. Action: turn off power before touching the dog or the appliance; get professional help immediately.

Nature's Hazards

If your outdoor activities include your Papillon, identify and avoid poisonous snakes, spiders, insects, toads, lizards, and porcupines. Any encounters with these dangers require veterinary treatment as soon as possible.

If a fishook is caught in her mouth or in a foot, cut off the barbed end and pull the hook through. Apply antiseptic to the wound.

Home Recipe for Eliminating Skunk Odor on Dogs
(courtesy of Sharon L. Vanderlip, D.V.M.)
Mix together:
1 quart 3-percent hydrogen peroxide
1/4 cup baking soda
1 teaspoon liquid soap
Bathe the dog with solution, avoiding the dog's eyes. Rinse thoroughly with tap water.

SHOW TIME! PAPILLONS DO IT ALL

If you have found your way to a dog show or match, you may have decided that your Papillon is far prettier, better behaved, or more agile than the other Papillons you saw. Bingo!—you have been bitten by the show bug.

Dog Shows and Other Options

Now that you have become interested in dog events, one of your first options is to decide whether you want to get involved in any of the show activities, and which activities appeal to you.

Dog Shows

Conformation shows evaluate dogs based on how closely they resemble the standard for their breed. Some shows are for all breeds, others are for specialties of one breed only. There are obedience trials and tracking, agility

Preparing a Papillon to participate in dog shows is relatively easy. Elaborate trimming is unnecessary, with regular brushing and sensible care contributing to giving your dog the competitive edge.

competitions, and team games. These are all companion events. There are performance events, such as field trials, but Papillons are not known to participate in these more rough-and-tumble activities.

All-breed shows: Shows occur just about every weekend of every year that offer classes for all of the breeds that are recognized by the administrative body, such as the AKC. Some of these shows have more than 3,000 dogs entered. Most of the dogs competing at these shows are competing for some of the 15 points needed for their championship.

Championship points: Points can be won by only one dog and one bitch in each breed at each show. The Winners Dog and Winners Bitch receive these points depending on the number of dogs in each sex competing in each breed at that show. If a dog or bitch wins Best of Breed or Group first, it can earn up to five points at a show. The number of points depends upon the number of entries in each sex in each breed. Wins of three, four, or five points are called major wins. Two majors must be won under two different judges before a championship can be awarded.

How Dogs Are Judged

In every breed of dogs males are judged first, then females (bitches). For each sex there are six classes:

1. Puppy—often divided between puppies that are 6 to 9 months and 9 to 12 months of age

2. Dogs 12 to 18 months of age

3. Novice for dogs that have not won more than three first-place blue ribbons in shows

4. Bred by Exhibitor for dogs, except Champions, that are owned and exhibited by the same person or kennel who are breeders of record with the AKC

5. American bred for dogs bred and born in the United States

6. Open for all dogs of any age; dogs from foreign registries must be shown in this class

The competitions: The first prize winners of each of the above classes compete for the winners class. Dogs of either sex that are champions plus the Winners Dog and Winners Bitch compete for the Best of Breed award. Whichever dog or bitch is awarded Best of Breed goes forward to compete in its appropriate group. Each of the seven group winners goes forward to compete for Best In Show.

The best of opposite sex prize is awarded to the dog or bitch that is considered by the judge to be the best specimen of the sex different from the Best of Breed winner. Either the Winners Dog or the Winners Bitch is designated as the better of the two and called Best of Winners.

What is judged: Each dog is judged on the judge's mental picture of the perfect dog of that breed, based on the breed standard and compares:

Physical structure, head, teeth, feet, bone structure, muscle tone

Condition, proper weight, condition of coat, attitude

Gait

Temperament

Fun Matches

Fun matches are like regular conformation shows except that no points are given toward a championship and champions are not allowed to compete. Matches are often held in the evening following Best In Show judging at all-breed shows. Do not take your Papillon to a fun match until you are sure he has had his proper vaccinations.

Papillons, like all toy dogs, are judged on a table. A puppy should receive regular table training to prepare for its future in the ring. And whether posing on the table or on the ground, a Papillon should always be the picture of alert elegance (inset).

When you go, talk to exhibitors and get some ideas about how Papillons should be groomed and presented. Ask club members about handling classes, which most clubs provide for a small fee to help people get ready to show their dogs.

Companion Events

If you want to go beyond the basics of training, there are several levels of formal training for your Papillon. At companion events, he can enter and earn certificates and titles of accomplishment. Training is like building blocks with steps that present increasing levels of difficulty and enjoyment for you and your dog. The AKC currently offers a ladder of training challenges.

Regular Classes

Novice obedience (companion dog)
Open obedience (companion dog excellent)
Utility and utility dog excellent
Obedience champion
National obedience champion
Versatile companion dog
Tracking and tracking dog excellent

Nonregular Classes

Graduate novice
Veterans class
Brace class
Team class

Other Programs

Canine good citizen
Agility
Prenovice obedience
Rally obedience

In Novice classes there are six exercises: heel on leash, stand for examination, heel free, recall, long sit, and long down. In Open there are seven exercises: heel free, drop on recall, retrieve on flat, retrieve over the high jump, broad jump, long sit, and long down (both of those with the handler away and out of sight). In Utility the exercises are signal exercise, scent discrimination, directed retrieve, directed jumping, and moving stand for examination. The sequence of exercises in Open B and Utility B vary at each trial according to random mixes prescribed by the AKC. Dogs can continue to compete to gain points toward an Obedience Championship based on the number of points awarded for first through fourth placements in Utility and/or Open classes. Once a year the top 25 Obedience Champions compete, and the one that wins each year is designated National Obedience Champion.

Basic Agility is fun and popular, although some competitors say that the courses are best done by Papillons that are larger than those permitted by the conformation breed standard. These are very fast-paced, timed runnings of obstacle courses involving jumping over objects, teetering on a seesaw, crossing a bridge, running through a tunnel, and weaving through upright poles. Titles can be earned in increasing levels of difficulty. Up-to-date descriptions of the events and titles available in Obedience and Agility can be obtained from the American Kennel Club or from their web site.

If your Papillon has had his proper basic training, including heeling, sitting, lying down, and staying, and if he has been well socialized and allowed to develop self-confidence, he will be able to pass the tests required to achieve a Canine Good Citizen certificate. He can also enter Prenovice and Rally Obedience competitions and will have success and fun there.

These Papillons are shown doing exercises in Agility competition. A mismark is jumping through the ring, while the other dog (who apparently conforms to the breed standard in regard to markings) is scaling the A-frame. Whatever they do, Papillons do it with zest.

Games and Fun Stuff

For strictly fun activities that are organized to meet the energy and interests of a Papillon, there are team sports such as fly-ball and drill teams.

Fly-ball is usually done in a team format and is based on the ability of the dogs to race down the length of the course, jump over obstacles, get to the ball dispenser, hit the release bar, catch a tennis ball, and race back to the starting line, where the next team member is then released to take off to do his performance. Time and accuracy are the measures of winning. Any activity in which speed and accuracy are required is just what your Papillon will love and in which he will excel.

Drill team competitions are usually at least four dogs, usually of the same breed, doing drill formats and exercises along with their handlers. The dogs often wear matching costumes, and the object is to have fun while doing the drill. Very often there is a clown that forgets the routine, but this would not be the Papillon. It would be too important to him to do what was expected and what would please the team captain. The clown, though, often gets the laughs and applause from the crowd, and that kind of attention might appeal to some Papillons. Drill teamwork is different from team competition in sanctioned show classes in conformation or obedience.

You and your Papillon can have a lot of fun with tricks. Teaching him to sit can be extended to having him sit up for his treat. Just keep raising the treat until he naturally rises up to get it. Then he is in a sit-up position. Good! Then he gets the treat. He will probably wave his paws while sitting up. With a little coaxing with your upraised palm you can turn this into a high-five response for another treat. The high five can also be taught after you teach your Papillon to shake. Until he is doing tricks reliably on command, remember to give him a treat any time he begins to show the behavior you want. When he is reliable, you can vary the times at which he gets a treat for doing the desired behavior.

Going one step further from sitting up, keep raising the treat until he is standing up on his hind legs. Dancing is made for Papillons. In fact, they are currently entering the world of canine freestyle in which the dog performs precision dance moves with his handler.

You can be as creative as you want as long as the tricks you are teaching him will not lead to broken bones or other injuries. Your Papillon will dream up games and tricks of his own to amuse you.

In the Service of Humankind

Papillons are exceptionally good at important kinds of service as long as the service requirements are within their physical and mental capabilities. One Papillon assistance dog would help his owner by getting into the clothes dryer to pull out the clothes she could not reach. Service includes going to convalescent hospitals and being therapy dogs, which is a specialty of the Papillon because their small size invites cuddling and their tendency to provide kisses is usually appreciated. Some Papillons are trained to be hearing ear dogs to assist deaf people. They are trained to alert their owners to the doorbell, the telephone, the smoke alarm, and dangers such as fire or smoke. Another program, Canine Companions for Independence, trains dogs to retrieve articles and do other helpful things that a disabled person cannot do for himself or herself. Papillons are quick but they are small, so they are limited in the size and weight of articles they can retrieve and they cannot pull a wheelchair. Being the owner of a certified therapy dog can

The Canine Good Citizen certificate is easy for a Papillon to obtain. All the dog needs is basic training and some self-confidence.

be as rewarding for you as it is for those people who get to hold and feel the warmth of your loving Papillon. (See "Information" for contacts to these programs.)

Versatile Papillons

For several years there has been a lady who shows her Papillons in conformation from her wheelchair. The dogs have been trained to heel by the side of the chair. When they come to the table for the judge's examination, the lady pats her lap, the dog jumps up into her lap and then onto the examination table. The dog exits the table in the same way and goes alongside the chair for its gaiting evaluation.

In obedience competition are Papillons that compete successfully by the side of their owners' wheelchairs. The dogs are able to complete all exercises as required by the regulations.

A Papillon in the Pacific Northwest helps his owner by working in the herding seminars she conducts. Ducks or kittens are just the right size to be herded by a Papillon.

These are examples of the adaptability and willingness to please characteristic of the Papillon.

INFORMATION

Registries

American Kennel Club, Inc.
Registration, Customer Service and
Companion Animal Recovery
5580 Centerview Dr., Ste. 200
Raleigh, NC 27606-3390
www.akc.org

American Kennel Club, Corporate Headquarters
260 Madison Avenue
New York, NY 10016
212-696-8200

The Canadian Kennel Club
89 Skyway Avenue, Ste. 100
Etobicoke, Ontario, Canada M9W 6R4
http://www.ckc.ca/

Federation Cynologique Internationale
Place Albert 1er, 13
B-6530 Thuin, Belgium
http://www.fci.be

The Kennel Club
1-4 Clarges Street, Picadilly
London W7Y 8AB, England

United Kennel Club (UKC)
100 E. Kilgore Road
Kalamazoo, MI 49002
269-343-9020
http://www.ukcdogs.com/

Parent Club

Papillon Club of America
Corresponding Secretary
http://www.papillonclub.org|

Canine Service Organizations

Delta Society (Therapy Dogs)
289 Perimeter Rd. E.
Renton, WA 98055-1329
www.deltasociety.org

Foundation for Pet Provided Therapy
P.O. Box 6308
Oceanside, CA 92058
760-630-4824

Therapy Dogs International
88 Bartley Road
Flanders, NJ 07836
http://www.tdi-dog.org

Canine Recreational Organizations and Information

North American Dog Agility Council, Inc.
HCR 2, Box 277
St. Maries, ID 83861
www.nadac.com

North American Flyball Association
1400 W. Devon Ave., #512
Chicago, IL 60660
www.flyball.org

World Canine Freestyle Organization
P.O. Box 350122
Brooklyn, NY 11235
718-332-8336

United States Dog Agility Association
P.O. Box 850955
Richardson, TX 75085-0995
www.usdaa.com

Medical and Health Organizations and Information

American Veterinary Medical Association
930 North Meacham Road
Schaumburg, IL 60173
www.avma.org

Burkholder, Craton R.
Emergency Care for Cats and Dogs: First Aid for Your Pet
New York, Michael Kesend Publishing, 1996.

CERF, Lynn Hall
Purdue University
Canine Eye Registration Foundation
625 Harrison Street
West Lafayette, IN 47907-2026
765-494-8179
canineeye@purdue.edu

Dodds, W. Jean, D.V.M.
"Changing Vaccine Protocols"
New York, *Dog News,* 2002.

National Animal Poison Control Center
Animal Product Safety Service
1717 South Philo Road, Suite 36
Urbana, IL 61802
888-426-4435
http://www.napcc.aspca.org

Orthopedic Foundation for Animals
2300 Nifong Boulevard
Columbia, MO 65201
www.ofa.com

First Aid Kits and Materials

http://www.first-aid-product.com/

www.caninemedicinechest.com

Identification and Recovery Information

Home Again Microchip Service
800-LONELY-ONE

National Dog Registry
P.O. Box 118
Woodstock, NY 12498-0116
800-637-3647

Petfinders
368 High Street
Athol, NY 12810
800-223-4747

Tattoo-A-Pet
1625 Emmons Avenue
Brooklyn, NY 11235
800-TATTOOS

Training References and Information

Crate Training Your Puppy, Woodland PetCare Centers, Tulsa, OK, undated.
Hodgson, Sarah, *Dog Tricks for Dummies,* Hungry Minds, Inc., 2001
Jester, Terry, *Living With Small and Toy Dogs, Training, Behavior and Personality Differences,* Alpine Publications, 1996.
"Training Your Puppy," Mission Viejo, CA, *Popular Dogs Series,* Topic Volume 3, 2001.
"Training for Agility," Mission Viejo, CA, *Popular Dogs Series,* Topic Volume 4, 2001.
www.patiopark.com

Leash training your Papillon puppy starts early and goes slowly but surely until she is accustomed to the leash.

above: This attractive puppy knows that the crate is its special place at home and a secure home away from home.

below: Dancing comes naturally to a Papillon. Its lovely, flowing coat makes it especially attractive as it gracefully moves on its hind legs.

Alternative Diets

Animal Food Services
Includes Kosher food
http://www.animalfood.com/

BARF (Bones and Raw Food or Biologically Appropriate Raw Food)

Cusick, William D., "Canine Nutrition and Choosing the Best Food for Your Breed of Dog," Aloha, OR, *The Animal Advocate,* Adele Publications, 1990.

Grognet, Jeff, D.V.M., "Nutrition—Commercial, Homemade and BARF, *Dogs in Canada,* April 2003, pp. 34–36.

http://www.animalwellnessmagazine.com/ magv3i3/natfood.htm

Natural Food—Wysong Archetype
www.epetpals.com/specialty_dog_food.htm

To look at this attractive group, it is easy to understand why the Papillon has always been considered the essence of elegance in dogs.

Important Note

This pet owner's manual tells the reader how to buy or adopt, and care for a Papillon. The author and publisher consider it important to point out that the advice given in this book is meant primarily for normally developed dogs of excellent physical health and good character.

Anyone who adopts a fully-grown dog should be aware that the animal has already formed its basic impressions of human beings. The new owner should watch the animal carefully, including its behavior toward humans, and should meet the previous owner.

Caution is further advised in the association of children with dogs, in meetings with other dogs, and in exercising the dog without a leash.

Even well-behaved and carefully supervised dogs sometimes do damage to someone else's property or cause accidents. It is therefore in the owner's interest to be adequately insured against such eventualities, and we strongly urge all dog owners to purchase a liability policy that covers the dog.

Not every Papillon can win in the show ring, but all can hold a loving place in someone's heart.

About the Author

Dr. Hungerland has been a judge of obedience since 1960 and of breeds since 1965. She now judges all Toys, all Non-Sporting, all Hounds, and all Sporting breeds. She has been a dedicated breeder and exhibitor of several breeds, most notably Poodles. She has been founder, officer, and active member of several all-breed and specialty dog clubs. Her devotion to the dogs extends to their people, as Dr. Hungerland is founder and President of the Dog Fancier's Fund, a charitable organization maintained to meet the needs of all fanciers. Dr. Hungerland is a Psychologist and is a retired member of the American Kennel Club Board of Directors, having been the first woman to have been elected to that body. In addition to many professional publications, she has been a contributing author of many articles and several regular columns of interest to dog lovers and fanciers. Dr. Hungerland has two grown children, four grown grandchildren, and four great-grandchildren, all of whom continue to delight and amaze her.

Photo Credits

Barbara Augello: 8 top, 8 bottom left and bottom right; Norvia Behling: 9 top, 12, 25 bottom, 29, 48, 77 bottom; Kent and Donna Dannen: 9 bottom right, 16 top, 17 bottom, 24 top, 33 bottom, 49, 53, 61, 64 top and bottom, 65 bottom, 72 bottom, 77 top; Isabelle Francais: 2, 4, 17 top, 20, 24 bottom, 28, 40, 56, 57; Nance Photography: 13, 16 bottom, 37, 41, 73; Pets by Paulette: 5, 9 bottom left, 21, 25 top, 32, 33 top, 36, 44, 45 top and bottom, 60, 65 top, 68, 69, 72 top, 76 top left, 76 top right, 76 bottom

Cover Photos

All photos by Norvia Behling.

Acknowledgments

I would like to thank the several Papillon breeders who responded to my inquiries cheerfully and with excellent information. Special thanks goes to Sharon Newcomb and Elyse Griffith, who met my endless questions and requests for review with the utmost patience. The devotion of Papillon fanciers to their breed has been refreshing and their encouragement has been appreciated completely.

I would also like to thank editor Seymour Weiss of Barron's Educational Series, Inc., whose time and assistance contributed significantly to the quality of the manuscript.

All inquiries should be addressed to:
Barron's Educational Series, Inc.
250 Wireless Boulevard
Hauppauge, NY 11788
http://www.barronseduc.com

International Standard Book No. 0-7641-2419-6

Library of Congress Catalog Card No. 2003045113

Library of Congress Cataloging-in-Publication Data
Hungerland, Jacklyn E.
    Papillons : everything about purchase, care, nutrition, behavior, and training / Jacklyn E. Hungerland ; illustrations by Michele Earle-Bridges.
        p. cm.
    ISBN 0-7641-2419-6
    1. Papillon dog. I. Title.

SF429.P2H85 2003
636.76—dc21   2003045113

Printed in China
9 8 7 6 5 4 3 2